In the Name of the Mother

Previously published by James Currey

Decolonising the Mind (1986)
NGŨGĨ WA THIONG'O

Moving the Centre (1993)
NGŨGĨ WA THIONG'O

Writers in Politics (1997 revised edition)
NGŨGĨ WA THIONG'O

Ngũgĩ wa Thiong'o
An Exploration of his Writing (1997 2nd edition)
DAVID COOK AND MICHAEL OKENIMKPE

Ngũgĩ wa Thiong'o Speaks (2006)
Interviews with the Kenyan Writer
REINHARD SANDER & BERNTH LINDFORS

In the Name of the Mother
Reflections on Writers & Empire

NGŨGĨ WA THIONG'O

**East African
Educational Publishers Ltd.**
Nairobi • Kampala • Dar es Salaam • Kigali

JC JAMES CURREY

James Currey
is an imprint of Boydell & Brewer Ltd
PO Box 9, Woodbridge,
Suffolk IP12 3DF (GB)
www.jamescurrey.com

and of
Boydell & Brewer Inc.
668 Mt Hope Avenue
Rochester, NY 14620-2731 (US)
www.boydellandbrewer.com

Published in Kenya by
E.A.E.P., PO Box 45314
Nairobi

The right of Ngũgĩ wa Thiong'o to be identified as
the author of this work has been asserted in accordance with
sections 77 and 78 of the Copyright, Designs and Patents Act 1988

British Library Cataloguing in Publication Data
A catalogue record for this book is available
on request from the British Library

ISBN 978-1-84701-084-1 James Currey (Paper)

The publisher has no responsibility for the continued existence or accuracy of URLs
for external or third-party internet websites referred to in this book,
and does not guarantee that any content on such websites is,
or will remain, accurate or appropriate.

Papers used by Boydell & Brewer are natural, recycled products
made from wood grown in sustainable forests.

Typeset in 12/14.5 Garamond
by Kate Kirkwood
Printed and bound in Great Britain
by CPI Group (UK) Ltd, Croydon CR0 4YY

Contents

Acknowledgement

I would like to thank Keith Sambrook who helped put this book together and Barbara Caldwell for her editorial input including making the index

Preface

These essays have roots in my personal history. On 12 December 1978 the Moi Dictatorship, in response to internal and international pressure, released me from a one-year imprisonment at Kamiti Maximum Security. But the regime ensured that I would not resume my job as Professor of Literature at the University of Nairobi. The imprisonment, without trial, had been a punitive act because of my novel, *Petals of Blood,* but more immediately my community based theatre work that produced *Ngaahika Ndeenda* (trs *I Will Marry When I Want*). The denial of a job was driven by the same motives: to keep me away from contact with students and regular working people.

Over the years, I had accumulated copious notes for the courses that I had given at the University of Nairobi on the European novel, and on African and Caribbean literature. I toyed with the idea of writing them as lectures, and distribute them freely, and thus defy and thwart the state's intent. This would not have earned me a coin but it would have been my way of fighting back, the way I had done in prison by writing *Caitaani Mũtharabainĩ/Devil on the Cross* on toilet paper. In the end I did not carry it out, less because the unsolicited lectures might have been interpreted as constituting subversive literature, anything in Kenya of the Moi days could have been so interpreted, but more because the struggle for daily survival as a lumpen-intellectual was hard enough. By 1982, I found myself an exile in Britain and later in the USA.

The idea of writing on individual authors and texts migrated with me and in between my work at Yale and New York University, and without my copious notes, which were still in Kenya, I started putting down my thoughts. By 1999 I had compiled some essays, sent them to James Currey, but with the hope that I would add more to the collection. Engagement in other scholarly and creative schemes took my attention away from the project. So, although I have included more recent essays, the majority of the essays in this collection are part of that unfinished project. Some of the essays are a continuation of my conversation with the work of George Lamming, Alex la Guma and Sembene Ousmane, but, unfortunately, the last two have passed on.

The collection is not as comprehensive as originally envisaged; still, it contains some of my thinking on the individual texts and themes. They are written in the spirit that counters the tendency to use texts as touchstones for general theory; the individuality of such texts and authors homogenised into evidence and proof of theory. But each text by a writer constitutes a world whose contours are worth exploring, its sites and sights worth savouring. Literary and critical theory would gain by being anchored in texts and close reading.

The literary texts that constitute modern African and Caribbean literature were written within or under the shadow of the empire. The languages used are those of the empire; the aesthetic of resistance emerges out of the general resistance to the empire and its consequences. Much of what goes under the term post-colonial literature remains bound to the empire by the language of use. Thus although there is no extended chapter on the concept and practice of the empire, the world of these essays and the texts on which they are based have been shaped by the practice of empire and that of resistance to it. For even when the physical empire has been forced to recede in the background, the metaphysical empire remains: colonial and postcolonial literature is in continuous struggle against the psychic pull of the metaphysical empire.

These essays contain the germ of the globalectical approach that I have recently theorized in my book: *Globalectics: Theory of the Politics of Knowing*.[1] They are not definitive; they are one person's view of the texts and authors. But I hope they contribute to the continuing discussions about the authors and texts and the aesthetic of resistance.

---

[1] Ngũgĩ wa Thiong'o, *Globalectics: Theory of the Politics of Knowing* (Columbia University Press, New York, 2012)

Birth of a Literature*
Heinemann, African Writers Series & I

Weep Not, Child (1964)
The River Between (1965)
A Grain of Wheat (1967)
The Black Hermit (1968) play
Secret Lives, and Other Stories (1975)
Petals of Blood (1977)
The Trial of Dedan Kimathi (1977) play
Detained: A Writer's Prison Diary (1981)
I Will Marry When I Want (1982) play
Devil on the Cross (1982)
Matagari (1987)

I have sometimes been accused of being a living contradiction for publishing with Heinemann in the African Writers Series. How can you, while denouncing imperialism, make a deal with a London-based publishing house that manufactures words harvested from Africa and African hands and then sells the finished product, the book, back to Africa at a profit? In what ways is this different from the similar process of gold, diamonds, copper, coffee, tea, all mined or grown in Africa, processed in the

---

* Based on a paper given at the ALA conference at La Jolla, in San Diego, April 2002 to celebrate forty years of the foundation of the African Writers Series in 1962. Thoughts were triggered by Brother Kamau Brathwaite asking me if anybody had ever written about Heinemann's relationship to colonialism, neocolonialism, postcolonialism.

1

West and sold back to Africa, the price of both the raw material and the finished product determined by the West? I am of course talking about the entire intellectual production, distribution and consumption of books, as mirroring that of the economic and political relationship of Africa to the West in general.

Heinemann Educational Books (HEB) and their unique product, the African Writers Series, have been part of my literary life and tonight I want to share with you aspects of the complex feelings evoked in me by the memory of the years of that relationship, 1962 to 2002. The fact is those years have seen some of the most joyful and painful moments in my life. Let me isolate two such moments which may also shed some light on the questions asked not only about my own relationship to the Series but the Series' own to relationship to events in postcolonial Africa.

The first moment is 1962. The December of the year before, that is 1961, I had just finished and delivered to a novel-writing competition the manuscript of what later became *The River Between* and immediately embarked on what later came to be *Weep Not, Child*.

Five months later, at the end of May 1962, under the firelight in a village in Kangemi, Kenya, some friends are trying to help type the half-finished manuscript for me. I am writing by hand, desperately trying to complete the novel, and they are desperately trying to finish typing whatever I am giving them. Why by fireside? There is no electricity in the area and we cannot afford paraffin oil, but we are committed to the task at hand. Why this desperation? Because I had been invited to a conference of African Writers of English Expression to be held in June at Makerere University College, Kampala, Uganda. Among the prospective attenders was Chinua Achebe. I had to show him the manuscript. It never occurred to me that he might not want, or even have the time, to read it. I had to show it to him, the author of *Things Fall Apart,* which had come out in 1958. He did not disappoint me and it was he who introduced my work to Heinemann. I have always appreciated the generosity of his spirit and more so when later I realised that he was then in the midst of writing *Arrow of God*. But can you imagine what I felt, when later the same year I got a letter from Heinemann, saying that they had accepted to publish the novel in their newly established African Writers Series with Achebe as the General Editor?

I was then in my third year, a student of English at Makerere – then an affiliate of the University of London. It was a period of optimism in East Africa and Africa in general. Tanganyika and Uganda had become independent following similar triumphs in Ghana, Nigeria and other parts of the continent. A year later, Kenya, which had gone through ten years of armed struggle against the British colonial state would follow suit.

There is a moment in the history of nations and peoples when spiritual and social production mirror and energise each other, and the fifties and early sixties was such a moment for Africa. The energy of the masses in their social struggle for independence and the general optimism must have found its way into the hands that held the pen. Let me use myself as an example.

Between 1961, two years after entering college, and 1964 when I graduated with honours, I had two novels *Weep Not, Child* and *The River Between*, accepted for publication in the African Writers Series, a three-act play *The Black Hermit*, performed at the Uganda National Theatre in Kampala, two one-act plays *The Rebels* and *The Wound in My Heart* performed at Makerere, eight short stories published in *Penpoint* and *Transition* and a couple of literary pieces in *Transition* and the Cape Town journal *The New African*, plus over eighty pieces in a regular column I used to run for the Nation group of Newspapers under the title 'As I See It'. I might add that I was the director of the same plays as well as being an assistant director to Nat Frothingham in a production of Shakespeare's

Macbeth in African costumes produced at Makerere. And still I seem to have had even more time on my hands because I had a one year stint as the Information Officer of the student's union, the Student's Guild, which included writing and editing their information bulletins, as well as activating other student journals like *Horizon*, and most important for me, was later to be appointed editor of *Penpoint*, a literary journal of the English Department at Makerere. The climax was the actual publication of *Weep Not, Child* in March 1964, a few weeks before the successful outcome of my degree exams.

On looking back, what amazes me about that period was not that I was able to do all that within five years of a full student life, but rather the fact that I took that as normal, as what a reasonably educated person could do, and this attitude coming from a person who grew up in a village community steeped in orature but hardly acquainted with books beyond a copy of shredded pages of the Bible. The literary 'deficiency' was corrected later in school, particularly at Alliance High School where for the first time I came across an actual library.[1] But I am saying this to set the context of the moment, 1962, the year of the emergence of the African Writers Series. My two novels *Weep Not, Child* and *The River Between* were an integral part of its early consolidation with Achebe's semi-trilogy of *Things Fall Apart, No Longer at Ease* and *Arrow of God* as a solid foundation of the Series.

As I headed to England to study and do research on the new emerging literature of the Caribbean with a focus on George Lamming, whose work I had encountered at Makerere, the future seemed clear. It was at Leeds University in 1965 that I started my third novel *A Grain of Wheat*. When it was published in the Series in 1967, it carried a prefatory statement that, while the events in the novel were fictitious, the situation of the drama was too real especially for the peasants who were seeing

---

[1] See my memoir, *In the House of the Interpreter* (New York: Random House 2012).

all they fought for being put to one side. This preface was only expressing the uneasiness felt in many writings of the period which saw, to borrow from Ayi Kwei Armah, that the 'beautyful ones' of the Independence era had not yet been born; a title echoed in Oginga Odinga's semi-autobiography *Not Yet Uhuru* also published in the Series. Both Armah in *The Beautyful Ones Are Not Yet Born* and Achebe in *A Man of the People*, published in the Series between 1966 and 1967, and had dramatised the coming of the era of coups and counter-coups and regional wars which were often proxies for the main combatants in the Cold War, the USA and the Soviet Union. My own novel *Petals of Blood*, written between 1970 and 1975 while teaching at Nairobi, Makerere, Northwestern University and Nairobi again, and published in the Series in 1977, was a thorough-going critique of the economic, political and cultural practices of what I had now come to recognise as a structural system: neocolonialism.

But even then I was sufficiently optimistic to have had an interesting face to face exchange with a South Korean diplomat who called on me at my offices of the Chair of Literature at the University of Nairobi to complain about what I had written on the then jailed Korean poet, Kim Chi Ha. Even worse that I had included his work in the literature syllabus. Kim Chi Ha had been jailed by the Park dictatorship on charges of furthering communism despite Kim Chi Ha's persistent claims that his conscience and practices were rooted in his faith as a Roman Catholic. The diplomat was trying to convince me that Kim Chi Ha was not really a writer, he was a political agitator under the cover of poetic words, and I recall ending the conversation with the cultural diplomat with the words, 'At least here in Kenya we do not imprison writers for their views.' I have always recalled the look that the diplomat gave me at the door, something between puzzlement and curiosity and disbelief. He probably had the last laugh when a few months after the publication of *Petals of Blood*, I was hauled into a maximum security prison.

Which brings me to the next moment that I want to share with you. It is once again the month of June but the year is 1982. Again I start with an invitation from Heinemann, this time to London, and the moment is pregnant with a mix of emotions. First I was going to London to help launch my books, *I Will Marry When I Want* (co-authored with Ngũgĩ wa Mĩriĩ), *Devil on the Cross* and *Detained*, due to be published in July in the African Writers Series. The three books were connected by the circumstances of their writing. *I Will Marry When I Want* was the play we developed with the Kamirithu village community in 1976-7 and which was stopped by the Kenya government a month before my arrest and imprisonment. *Devil on the Cross* was the novel I wrote in prison on toilet paper. *Detained* was my prison memoir based on notes I took in my cell, and the theme of the memoir is really about the circumstances of my imprisonment and of writing as resistance.

But what most unites the three is the issue of African languages. *I Will Marry When I Want* was originally in Gĩkũyũ (*Ngaahika Ndeenda*), a fact which may have led to me being sent to prison in the first place. I say this because when the Heinemann branch in Kenya agreed to publish the novel *Caitaani Mũtharabainĩ*, the publisher Henry Chakava, after getting several threatening phone messages was later attacked outside his home a week before the publication date. Actually they wanted to abduct him in the boot of their car, but when this failed they hacked off one of his fingers and it had to be re-sewn, a saga that the publisher told in an article in Charles Cantalupo's book *Ngũgĩ wa Thiong'o: Texts and Contexts*.

As further confirmation of the regime's hostility to African languages my play *Mother Sing for Me,* also in Gĩkũyũ, was stopped. They outlawed the Kamirithu community theatre group, then sent three truckloads of heavily armed police to raze the Kamirithu open air theatre to the ground.

That was in March 1982, and here I am, June the same year, on my way to London to help launch the English language translations of these texts, and the sentiments of hope were not dissimilar to those I had when in June 1962 I had embarked on a train to Kampala for the Conference of African Writers of English Expression and ended up connecting with Heinemann who now had become publishers of both my Gĩkũyũ language texts and their English translations. I would come back home energised to do more.

But I never returned to Kenya. A week before I was to leave London for Kenya, I learnt that I was due for arrest, detention or possible elimination should I return. And indeed two of the people I worked with at Kamirithu had fled the country a few hours ahead of the police squad sent to arrest one and, in the case of Ngũgĩ wa Mĩriĩ, to eliminate the other. Heinemann publishers and the African Writers Series were now stuck with me. Instead of their taking care of a temporary guest at the hundred dollar a night Hotel Russell, they were now hosting a political fugitive with an uncertain future at a flat at the back of their offices in Bedford Square. So it was as a guest of the African Writers Series in London in 1982 that I started my life in exile, an option which I had completely rejected and said so in my book *Detained*.

I believe that the invitation to launch the books in London saved my life; that had I stayed in Kenya, I would not have survived the repression that followed the failed August Airforce coup of 1982. I was spared courtesy of Heinemann and able to continue to tell the tale and champion the cause of African languages in theory and practice.

In terms of my literary tribulations, my experiences in one form or another will be echoed by others, most of whom are in the Series. I am thinking here of writers and editors like Rajat

Neogy, Peter Nazareth, Bahadur Tejani, John Ruganda, Okot p'Bitek from Uganda; Wole Soyinka from Nigeria, Jack Mapanje from Malawi and of course several more from apartheid-era South Africa. Death, imprisonment, exile have been the lot of the African writer since the heyday of the Conference of African Writers of English Expression in Kampala in 1962.

Somehow I have kept hope alive in me through my writings. *Matigari* was published in 1986 in Kenya by Henry Chakava's East African Publishing House (formerly Heinemann Kenya) and then was immediately arrested and banned by the same Kenyan regime. It is not without pride that I can say I have, as of 10 March 2002, finished what I am calling my magnum opus, *Mũrogi wa Kagogo. The Wizard of the Crow*, as it is called in its English translation, is an ambitious project which tries to sum up, from Africa's perspective, the twentieth century in the context of the emergence of modernity from colonial capitalism to present-day globalisation. It has taken me over five years to write and I had hoped that there was a place for such a long novel in the African Writers Series.[2]

In the brochure released by Heinemann to mark their forty years of the African Writers Series you will find my claim, which is a repeat of what I have said before in some of my writings, that African literature in European languages is the nearest thing we have to a Pan-African common literary inheritance. The African Writers Series has published writers from virtually every country in Africa thus enabling a dialogue among readers and writers from the three main colonial traditions: Portuguese, French and English. They have also enabled a dialogue between Africans of the continent and the diaspora. A Pepetela, a Sembene, an

---

[2] Heinemann did not publish it. But Henry Chakava did publish both the Gĩkũyũ edition (in 2004) and later its English translation, from the Nairobi publishing house, which was by then known as East African Educational Publishers (EAEP). The American edition of *The Wizard of the Crow* was published by Pantheon and the UK edition by Harvill Secker (both in 2006).

Achebe, a Soyinka, a Mahfouz, an Ama Ata Aidoo, belong to Kenya and Uganda as much as they do to Angola, Senegal, Nigeria, Egypt and Ghana. You have only to see the reverence with which African writers are held in every part of the continent to realise the validity of the claim. I can testify to that. I have been stopped in the streets of Zimbabwe, Ghana, Nigeria, by people who have never met me before to say what my books have meant to them. It is not even the words: sometimes the light in their eyes tells all.

When I visited South Africa for the first time in 1991 Nelson Mandela, then the President of ANC, gave me an audience at the party's Headquarters in Johannesburg, and for slightly more than an hour, he talked gratefully about what the work of African writers meant to him when on Robben Island. All the writers and works he cited were in the African Writers Series, not to mention that his own work *No Easy Walk to Freedom* was also part of the series, as was the work of Kwame Nkrumah and Kenneth Kaunda before him.[3]

Rightly or wrongly, the Series may be accused of ghettoisation or being part of a neocolonial enterprise and its foundation does indeed coincide with Africa's transition from colonial to neocolonial relationship with the West. But the commitment of the founding and later editors, Van Milne, Alan Hill, Keith Sambrook, Aig Higo, James Currey, Henry Chakava, Vicky Unwin and Becky Clarke was deep and serious. They established something close to a community of writers.

In generating challenges the Series has also inspired a lot of indigenous African publishing as part of Africa's continuing struggle for cultural identity and independence. The Series has also made possible a vast and vigorous literary scholarship in

---

[3] The current generation of African writers, Chimamanda Ngozi Adichie, Helon Habila, Mukoma wa Ngũgĩ, to mention a few only, were raised on authors in the Series.

Africa and the world, an integral part of the theoretical and critical inquiries of the modern and postmodern, which now goes under the name of postcolonial studies.

I am grateful that the books, the writers and the Series are there to provoke debate, emulation, challenge, accusations even, and I am glad to be part of the celebration of the forty years of its existence, which also coincides with forty years of my writing career.

PUBLISHER'S BIBLIOGRAPHIC NOTE

For the record, within a year of Ngũgĩ having given this celebratory address in April 2002 the management of Heinemann made the unexpected announcement that 'no new titles would be added to the Series for the foreseeable future'. Becky Clarke went to found Ayebia Publishers to continue to publish literature from Africa. In 2008 Heinemann was taken over by Pearson which already owned Longman. Thanks to the initiative of Alex Moore and other staff at Longman new titles began to appear again in the African Writers Series in 2012, the fiftieth anniversary of the Series. There is a section on 'Publishing Ngũgĩ' (pp. 112-140) in James Currey *Africa Writes Back: The African Writers Series and the Launch of African Literature* (James Currey, EAEP, HEBN, Weaver Press, Wits University Press, Mkuki na Nyota and Ohio University Press 2008).

In the Name of the Mother
Lamming & the Cultural Significance of 'Mother Country' in the Decolonisation Process[1]

George Lamming *In the Castle of My Skin* (London: Michael
    Joseph 1953; New York: McGraw Hill 1953; Reprint with
    new Introduction New York: Schocken 1983)
—— *The Emigrants* (London: Michael Joseph 1954; New York:
    McGraw Hill 1955)
—— *The Pleasures of Exile,* non-fiction (London: Michael
    Joseph 1960)
—— *Season of Adventure* (London: Michael Joseph 1960)
—— *Water with Berries* (Harlow: Longman 1971)

> I can understand our missionaries going to Africa and the West
> Indies... they need what they're being told . . . But it's the strangest
> thing to me such people leaving their own people to go to England
> to do what's most needed in their home.[1]

> Why the hell a man got to leave where he born when he ain't theif
> not'n, nor kill nobody, an' to make it worse to go somewhere he
> don't like . . . 'Cause I'll tell you somet'ing, if there's one place under
> de sun I hate like poison, 'tis that said England.[2]

> Today I shudder to think how a country, so foreign to our own
> instincts, could have achieved the miracle of being called mother.[3]

---

[1] George Lamming *The Emigrants* (London: Michael Joseph 1954; New York: McGraw
    Hill 1955, p. 73).
[2] Ibid., p. 37.
[3] George Lamming, 'Introduction' to reissue *In The Castle of My Skin* (New York: Schocken
    1983, p. xii).

The relationship between the coloniser and the colonised in Africa and Asia started as a one-way flow of human traffic from the home of the coloniser, usually portrayed as the mother country, to the home of the colonised, that is to say, the colony. But post-World War II there was a counter-flow of human traffic from colonial territories to the 'mother' countries, a phenomenon summed up in Salman Rushdie's notion of the empire striking back. This phenomenon continues in the postcolonial era so that today in the homes of all the former colonial and semi-colonial powers there are sizable populations from the former colonies. Nowhere is that counter-flow of human traffic better illustrated than in that historic emigration of West Indian workers, students, writers, intellectuals of all sorts, to Britain in the 1950s. That generation of counter-emigrants, are the parents and grandparents of the Black Britons who came of age in the Thatcherite era and who voted in, for the first time, their Black representatives to the erstwhile all-white mother of parliaments. But it was part of a historical trend. In all the homes of the former colonial powers the empire is striking back in every area of economic, political and cultural life. The question of why and its implications, a puzzle to both the coloniser and the colonised, still looms large in postcolonial politics, theory and practice. In *The Pleasures of Exile*, and describing the journey which brought him and his fellow writers to England, the Barbajan writer, George Lamming, who was part of the first wave of flight to the England of the fifties, has talked of his fellow emigrants as a people largely in search of work. 'During the voyage we had got to know each other very well. The theme of the talk was the same. It had to do with some conception of a better break.'[4] Can the phenomenon be adequately described in terms of economics alone when in fact the majority ends up at the bottom of the economic ladder? And still they come even in

[4] George Lamming *The Pleasures of Exile* (London: Michael Joseph 1960, p. 212).

the postcolonial era? George Lamming has made that question and its implications, in the context of the relationship between the coloniser and the colonised, central to his work. In the process, Lamming finds it necessary to hold a dialogue with Shakespeare. The English bard was there at the rosy dawn of capitalism with its roots in slavery and colonialism. The contradictions in western modernity which begins with the loot and plunder of other peoples are reflected in his work. Lamming was there at the sunset of capitalism in its colonial form. Capitalism had already bloomed into imperialism engulfing the whole globe but it was being challenged everywhere. Western modernity was turning into postmodernity and colonialism into postcolonialism. The modern and the postmodern are thus rooted in colonialism. In looking at Shakespeare, Lamming is examining the beginnings of it all. The key text is *The Tempest*. In this text, Prospero has left his home to occupy Caliban's island. In Lamming's texts, Caliban is constantly going back to the home of Prospero. Lamming has stated, in *The Pleasures of Exile*, that the subject of his works was the emigration of the West Indian Writer, as a colonial and exile, from his native kingdom once inhabited by Caliban to the tempestuous island of Prospero and his language. What is it that so fascinates Caliban in the home of Prospero?

In an interview published in *Black World* shortly after the issue of his two novels, *Water with Berries* and *Natives of My Person*, Lamming talked about Caliban's relationship to Prospero's language, as a contract. Once Caliban had accepted the language, or was even forced to accept it, his development would always be 'inextricably tied with that pioneering aspect' of the coloniser. 'Caliban, at some stage would have to find a way of breaking that contract which got sealed by language, in order to restructure some alternative reality for himself.'[5] 'Concealed in and by

---

[5] George E. Kent, 'A Conversation with George Lamming', *Black World*, 1973, vol. XXII, no. 5, p. 89.

language' was another contract, a contract with the idea of the home which had produced that language. For the colonised, his first encounter with the home of the coloniser is through its definition in the language learned, in the books read, in the stories told, in the pictures painted, hints expressed in so many ways, all pointing to the home as the source of everything that is good and noble in contrast to Caliban's savage environment and being. The country that sent out these emissaries of light to the dwellers in Plato's dark cave, how much more luminous must be the light that bathed its sky?

In his first novel, *In the Castle of My Skin*, Lamming, showed how the classroom had shaped the idea of big England and Little England in the imagination of Barbajan children. Barbados was the Little England to the Big England which was also Great Britain, the home base of the Empire. The idea, planted in the colonial classroom, haunts the world of all Lamming's novels from *In the Castle of My Skin* to *Water with Berries*. In this last novel, set almost entirely in England, the characters are exiles from the upheavals of a postcolonial situation foreseen with so much clarity in *Season of Adventure*. The England in which they live is no longer the home base of a world power. Its influence on the Caribbean has been supplanted by what the narrative describes as the big neighbour to the North. The characters may have grown with the idea of England, the mother country as a refuge but, according to Lamming, 'they are experiencing in their consciousness the disintegration of that idea, the irrelevance and the falsity of that idea beside the hitherto obscured reality.'[6] The characters in *Water with Berries* published in 1971 are revisiting and traversing a territory earlier visited and trodden by the generation of the 1950s, a time when much of the Caribbean is still under direct colonial rule and the territory of the novel *The Emigrants* that Lamming published in 1960.

[6] Ibid.

That the contract with the idea of the home of the coloniser is a much more active force in people's lives is borne out by the testimony of other writers and sources. An extract from *To Sir with Love*, the 1959 autobiographical narrative of E.R. Braithwaite from the then British Guyana, makes the point. In the narrative, Braithwaite, describes how he grew up with the idea of the British, he and others literally becoming British in every way, their being shaped by an idea transmitted from generation to generation:

> Myself, my parents and my parents' parents, none of us knew or could know any other way of living, of thinking, of being; we knew no other cultural pattern, and I had never heard any of my forbears complain about being British.[7]

E.R. Braithwaite was an RAF pilot for the British during the Second World War. England may have been wounded in the Second World War but it is still the home base of the Empire. The idea was so active that in the 1950s it literally drew thousands of Caribbeans out of their lives on the islands in pursuit of the England of their childhood memories, dreams and hopes. In the minds of the emigrants, before their arrival, England was still that idea, implanted in the colonial classroom, of a mother who cared[8]

---

[7] E.R. Braithwaite *To Sir with Love* (The Four Square Edn, p. 31). See also Jamaica Kincaid article, 'On Seeing England For the First Time', in *Transition* Magazine no. 51. She recounts how the map of England had impacted on her when as a child in school she was asked to draw it. 'I did not know then that the statement, "draw a map of England" was something far worse than a declaration of war, for in fact already a flat-out war would have put me on alert, and again in fact, there was no need for war – i had long ago been conquered. I did not know then the statement was part of a process that would result in my erasure, not my physical erasure, but my erasure all the same. i did not know then that this statement was meant to make me feel in awe and small whenever i heard the word "England": awe at its existence, small because i was not from it. I did not know very much of anything then – certainly not what a blessing it was that i was unable to draw a map of England correctly.'

[8] The characters in the novels of Samuel Selvon are also attracted to England by both economic necessity and the idea. Johnie Sobert in Andrew Salkey's novel, *Escape to an Autumn Pavement*, rebels against a middle-class upbringing expressed in a kind of Britishness.

and this is what Lamming sets out to explore in *The Emigrants*.

The emigrants who include teachers, writers, students and workers come from almost every island then governed by Britain. They are all in the same ship literally and metaphorically. For whatever their island of origins, whatever their vocations, and whatever their individual motives, their lives are linked together in the common feeling summed up by one of the characters as a search for that better break that Lamming himself talks about in *The Pleasures of Exile*. England is their common hope for that break. But it is still England which is more an idea than a reality. They fall into two main groups: the workers and students in one; and middle-class intellectuals and professionals in the other.

Included in the first group of *The Emigrants* are all those who hope to get jobs and at the same time educate themselves to acquire some kind of profession – 'anything you can get some papers for an' go back home...an' make a good an' proper livin.'[9] Higgins for instance intends to go to a school in Liverpool for six months or year's training as a cook. He has big ambitions for the children he has left behind and he wants to give them 'education an' qualifications an' distinction.'[10] Their search for papers is therefore also linked to a conception of self-worth: papers and qualifications are an outward sign that a person has put god-given talents to some purpose: at old age, the person can look back and be proud of having spent 'the time God give you well an' proper.'[11] The echo of the biblical story about the five talents is relevant to their social situation: the man with the five talents is condemned, not because his talents are small or limited, but because he did not use them fruitfully. For the Caribbean worker, purposeful living is to be measured by how far a person has climbed away from the surrounding deplorable

[9] *The Emigrants*, p. 59.
[10] Ibid., p. 60.
[11] Ibid., p. 59.

social conditions. England is seen as offering a chance to trade a person's talents fruitfully, a chance denied to them by the colonial underdevelopment of the island countries of their origins.

The other group of emigrants is largely of middle-class upbringing and education. For a variety of personal reasons, they want to escape what they consider a restrictive and suffocating atmosphere in the islands of their various origins. There is the 'I' narrator, who could be Lamming or the equivalent of the Boy G of *In the Castle of My Skin* who feels that the personal freedom felt on first entering Trinidad from Barbados, was finished. He describes this freedom as having been fresh and precious, like a child's freedom or that of some emancipated colonial. But after four years in Trinidad, he feels a desire to get out into a wide world. England is that world. In this psychological category fall people like Dickinson, a schoolteacher, whose mouth is set into a permanent scowl, and who would not mix with the workers. His middle-class snobbery gets only momentarily satisfied when he is talking to white people on board. He is in a permanent nervous condition because of the fact that he is really in flight from his skin colour. He lives in mortal terror of the possibility of people seeing through him to the hollow man within. Miss Bis is running away for similar reasons, really escaping from the consequences of her attitudes to skin pigmentation. She had broken an engagement with a dark-skinned doctor in favour of a white man she barely knows and who in turn jilts her on the wedding day. She becomes the subject of a calypso. The shame is too great for her to remain at home. She now wants to forget the past and graft herself to a new stem which is England itself.

Though the two groups are separated by their social and educational positions, they are all involved in a similar flight from the social and psychological limitations of the past. They are equally unsure about the future. But it is the common historical experience they share which is the basis of their individual and

collective uncertainties about the past and the present; and also
of their hopes for a future made possible by the fact of England.
'Flight, we're all in flight'[12] says Collis, and this is what makes
him see clearly what really connects him to the group. The
ship acquires a symbolic significance: it is the whole Caribbean
territory, and the journey, is a voyage of discovery into their
Caribbean identity. Their contract with English and the idea of
England is a common bond. Initially they don't know it. They are
all, objectively, Caribbeans, but they have to know it. They have
to come to a knowledge of it, to become aware of it, to own it,
and the talks and interactions in the ship help generate that self-
awareness of their common origins, experience and hope. As
Tornado puts it:

> We got to suffer first and then come together. If there is one thing
> England going to teach all o' we is that there ain't no place like home
> no matter how bad home is. But you got to pay to learn an' believe
> me I may not see it but those comin' after goin' to make better
> West Indian men for coming' here an' seein' for themselves what
> is what.[13]

Being is one thing; becoming aware of it is a point of arrival
by an awakened consciousness and this involves a journey. This
process of becoming is what is dramatised in *The Emigrants* particularly in the actions that take place in the ship.

When the emigrants first gather for talk, they are full of
chauvinistic views about their own places of origin. They vie
with one another enumerating the virtues of their individual
islands. The Barbajan for instance is categorical about his island
having the best climate and education. The Grenadian claims,
for his island, the best beaches and the best socialist party. It's
the man they call The Governor, a person of wide travel and

---

[12] Ibid., p. 49.
[13] Ibid., p. 76.

experience, who shatters their narrow views.

To him they are all 'blasted small islanders'. 'All them', he tells them, were his brothers and he warns them against what he calls the 'monkey talk about big island an' small island.'[14] He challenges them to look into themselves: the islands they are leaving behind, the unknown to which they have all committed themselves, and even their motives for leaving. It is in the process of doing so that they discover their similar aspirations arising from their common bond of their past colonial experience. The Jamaican best articulates their new feelings when he argues that the water between the islands do not separate them. 'Different man, different land, be de same outlook. Dat's de meaning o' West Indies'.[15] Their present venture, the search for a better break, is symbolic of a new nation's need to prove its ability to create and to act. People and nations are always proving something to themselves. This is truer in the Caribbean context where people view themselves as a 'complete new generation of race almighty Gawd create yesterday'[16] and therefore are more sensitive about who they are. They want to prove and assert their identity. If you asked them what they want to prove, 'the answer sound stupid. They want to prove that them is themself.'[17] The Caribbean experience has a universal dimension: to strive; struggle is the basis of human progress and identity. 'The interpretation me give hist'ry is people the world over always searchin' an feelin', from the time immemorial, them keep searchin' an' feelin'[18] The ship and the voyage then function as catalysts for a collective self-awareness as West Indians, a tremendous experience and prerequisite before they can meaningfully meet the challenges of

[14] Ibid., p. 39.
[15] Ibid., p. 39.
[16] Ibid., p. 65.
[17] Ibid., p. 65.
[18] Ibid., p. 66.

the wider world they are about to enter. The Barbajan who has been the most chauvinistic at the beginning of the voyage best articulates the new vision of a shared Caribbean identity:

> You say a marvelous thing 'bout provin' something. It makes me feel that I really belong to something bigger than myself. I'd feel now that whatever happen to you or you or you wus happening to me an' the said way round.[19]

Thus whatever their individual responses, they will be experiencing the reality of the idea of England as West Indians. This, in itself, is not the answer to the problems each individual will experience. For while they enter Britain with a new awareness of themselves as West Indians, and during their exile, they will orbit around the same social centres, each individual will encounter shattering experiences, and how deeply a person is lacerated by them depends ultimately on their individual sensitivity, stamina and outlook on life and thought. There are, of course, things that they suffer as foreigners; as Caribbeans and as workers in a race conscious and class-structured society. But their West-Indianness is put into relief in their relationship with other peoples, for instance, continental Africans and the English.

The African in the narrative is presented as being more confident and more sure of himself than his West Indian counterpart. He is mysterious, at times cunning and arrogant, but this springs from his confidence. Azi, the African, is for instance contrasted with Dickinson, the West Indian school teacher, to the disadvantage of the latter. If Azi speaks English with a correctness that is almost fastidious, it is because, for him indeed, English is a language learnt from text books unlike the affectation of Dickinson who was born into the language. The African is not in as much need to prove himself. When the barber speaks of the need for West Indians to prove that they are as good as those who ruled over them, Azi retorts that the need to prove oneself assumes that 'at the moment you don't believe you are.'[20] Although Azi in *The Emigrants* is not a political activist, he is the one depicted as having the self-confidence to make all sorts of connections. In the sections of the novel that follow the arrival in England and residence in London, Azi emerges as the main link in the chain of events that affect most of the characters. Lamming attributes this to the African relationship to his culture and certainly to his experience of freedom. The positive depiction of the African presence was obviously affected by the anti-imperialist mood of optimism sweeping through Africa at the time.

The Emigrants is written at a time when the struggle for independence in Africa is intensifying, best symbolised by Kwame Nkrumah and the Convention Peoples Party in the Gold Coast. In Kenya and Algeria there were armed struggles. Everywhere on the continent were calls and militant marches for freedom. The Gold Coast became independent as Ghana in 1957. In 1958 George Lamming visited Ghana where he spent some time with an Ashanti family.

As Lamming has written of Ghana in *The Pleasures of Exile*,

> here one saw the psychological significance of freedom. It does something to a man's way of seeing the world. It is an experience which is not gained by education or money, but by an instinctive re-evaluation of your place in the world, an attitude that is the logical by-product of political action. And again one felt the full meaning, the full desecration of human freedom contained in the word colonial. One felt that the West Indian of my generation was truly backward, in this sense. For he was not only without this experience of freedom won; it was not even a vital force or need in his way of seeing himself and the world which imprisoned him.'[21]

[20] Ibid., p. 133.
[21] *The Pleasures of Exile*, p.165. In the interview with George Kent published in *Black World* Lamming says that it was during the stay that he was shown a postcard of the family with whom he was staying. 'These are all natives of my person,' he was told in

The African presence in the narrative is used to highlight the West Indian debilitating obsession with the idea of England. In their encounter with the African, the Caribbean characters are shown as evasive, suspicious, and sometimes reacting to that presence as if they have internalised English racism, thus practicing on the continental African the same prejudices under which they themselves have suffered under the English. At a hair dresser's shop run by a West Indian, the girls pass derisive comments on their own boys who go out with the English treating them to everything 'and you'll never find an Englishman to even look in our direction'[22]. Yet the same lot speak of Azi in derogatory terms. Imagine Azi in any of the West Indian islands, they gossip, 'why he'd be the laughing stock of the town with all of them funny marks on his face.'[23] An African girl, Krawnaula, actually Aziz's cousin, comes to the shop to have her hair done and Miss Docking refuses to serve her, 'You must not think I have something against you but I do it for my friends,' she is told. While in the narrative there are reasons why Miss Docking should act suspiciously – for one, the premises are not licensed, she runs the business illegally – she is nevertheless depicted as reacting to the African girl with an inbred irrational fear. In *The Pleasures of Exile* Lamming seems to argue that this fear stems from the West Indian's faulty education about Africa which did not provide him with any reading to rummage through as 'a guide to the lost kingdoms of names and places which give geography a human significance.' He knows the continent through rumour and myth

(contd) reference to the children. Many years later this was to form the title of his novel, *The Natives of My Person*. The incident shows how real historical events do force their way into Lamming's imagination as he writes. In *In The Castle of My Skin* he had shown that he was very much aware of world events and that he could write about them even where he did not have a direct personal experience. Trumper for instance is depicted as having visited the USA and experienced pan-africanism even though Lamming at the time of writing had not yet been to America.

22 *The Emigrants*, p. 153.
23 Ibid., p. 153.

propagated by the coloniser, and through the gradual conditioning of his education, he comes to identify Africa with fear, 'a fear of that continent as a world beyond human intervention.'[24] The negative depiction of Africa and blackness and the past of the Afro-Caribbean and indeed of other regions outside the 'mother country' contribute to, and intensify, the mystification of the idea of England. The negative dark otherness of Africa contributes to the luminous ideal which is Britain, an ideal that includes the contours of her history, geography, architecture and the quality of motherly care.

In England, Lamming wrote in *The Pleasures of Exile*, the West Indian student did not need to try to understand an Englishman, 'since all relationships begin with an assumption of previous knowledge, a knowledge acquired in the absence of the people known. This relationship with the English is only another aspect of the West Indian relation to the idea of England'.[25] In the West Indian consciousness, Lamming wrote in the introduction to the 1983 Schocken edition of the *In the Castle of My Skin*, 'empire was not a very dirty word, and seemed to bear very little relation to those forms of domination we now call imperialist.'[26]

One aspect of this idea is that England is the land of opportunity, as 'heritage and a place of welcome'.[27] This is very graphically and forcefully dramatised through the consciousness of Collis. In *The Emigrants* as the boat which brings the voyage to an end at the Albion shores at Liverpool, his thoughts fly with anticipation:

> He saw the land, England. There was something beyond the porthole. There was life, life, life, and wherever there was life there

---

[24] *The Pleasures of Exile,* p. 160.
[25] Ibid., p. 160. For this reason, Lamming thinks it would be beneficial for West Indians to go and study in a different European country.
[26] *In the Castle of My Skin,* p. xii.
[27] Ibid.

had to be something, something other than no-THING which did not matter. It mattered to be in England.[28]

What he reads in a newspaper about housing shortage and unemployment does not worry him at this moment of arrival; it does not interfere with the idea of England and her benevolence. The report does not matter because

> there beyond the water too large for his view was England rising from beneath her anonymous surface of grey to meet a sample of the men who are called her subjects and whose only certain knowledge said that to be in England was all that mattered.[29]

'It is the measure of our innocence,' Lamming recalls that period in the introduction to the 1983 Schocken edition of the *In The Castle of My Skin*, 'that neither the claim of heritage nor the expectation of welcome would have been seriously doubted. England was for us not a country with classes and conflicts of interests like the islands we had left. It was the name of a responsibility whose origin may have coincided with the origin of time.'[30]

Another aspect of the idea, almost contradictory, is the view in *The Emigrants* of the English as a hostile race. The English people are seen as out to 'squeeze a man like me any day they see him'; they don't like West Indians in their country and are only interested in driving them back to the islands, as if they, the English 'ever stay where they live'. If you become prosperous, 'they make a point o' pushin' the enemy, 'an if you doan' keep yuh eye open for when they ready to stab you in the back you'll end up bad so.'[31] This being the case it calls for the West Indian emigrants to remain alert, suspicious, and keep the right company. Above all they must not be deceived by the Englishman's smile for

---

[28] *The Emigrants*, pp. 106-7.
[29] Ibid.
[30] *In the Castle of My Skin*, p. xii.
[31] *The Emigrants*, p. 67.

it has teeth that can bite. So in a way England is also the land of the enemy and the manner of dealings with an enemy are always dictated by tactical necessity. The West Indian must survive, in this land of the enemy, by outwitting and out-maneuvering the English. So the idea of England is a complex of contradictory attitudes and emotions.

The idea of England, the two aspects mostly, is of course modified by their encounter with reality. Soon the emigrants are revolted by the physical environment; baffled by the social habits of the English and especially what they consider the coldness of the English: no talking till you talked; no speaking till you spoke, 'no notice till you notice, no nothing till something'. In a comic scene in the house of the Pearsons, Collis takes refuge in a lavatory to escape from the restraint and the cold formality of the house. 'He would like to have kicked him in the stomach, not in anger, but as a way of evoking some genuine emotion. Only violence could make Mr Pearson feel.'[32] Alas! Mother England does not welcome her subjects with open arms and a smiling face; 'why do you people come here?'[33] The tone in their speech is patronising: 'you people speak excellent English for a foreigner. Much better than the French.'[34]

The emigrants literally and metaphorically go through the English fog into their various encounters with the reality which they now experience both as a group and as individuals. Collectively they have difficulties in finding jobs. England after all is not the land of opportunity where the emigrants can make a better economic break. The appalling social conditions reduce some like Lillian to pawn the clothes of a friend. Higgins who had talked so hopefully of qualifications and papers finds that the school for cookery has closed. Within two weeks after arrival

---

[32] Ibid., p. 147.
[33] Ibid., p. 115.
[34] Ibid., p. 117.

he is held by the police on the suspicion of pedalling drugs. He is actually innocent. The shock drives him mad and towards the end of the narrative we find him desperately trying to stowaway back home. Miss Bis who has come to England to escape her past, changes her name Ursula Bis to Una Solomon, is involved in a lesbian relationship with Peggy, an English woman, and later, murders another emigrant, her own friend, Queenie. And as Una Solomon trying to escape her past, she ends up in the hands of Frederick, the ex-colonial white, the very person who had jilted her. Only she does not recognise him, the implication being that one cannot escape from one's past. Dickinson who in the ship would not talk with the group and would only seek the company of white people on board, is finally humiliated by an English couple who lure him into undressing only to discover that their only desire – which he has mistaken for the woman's love for him – is actually to see his nakedness. And more, they had invited their friends for this show of black nudity. The consciousness of the invasion of his body by all those anthropological eyes is so intense that he almost shares the same crazed fate with the Higgins from whom he had tried to establish social distance during the voyage. In the end, he is seen seeking out the company of the very group he had earlier rejected. He desperately wants to make peace with them and be admitted into their lives as way of restoring himself to his violated body. 'He had to be assured that he was still there under his clothes, inside his skin, and these were possibly the only people who could probably restore the life, the identity, which the eyes of others had drained away.'[35] Phillips, the student, finds himself in a painful dilemma. He gets a girl pregnant but to let her have his child would mean his loss of scholarship and all the hopes of an academic qualification. But remembering that he himself had been born out of wedlock, he recoils from the reality of an

[35] Ibid., p. 268.

abortion: what right has he to deny another life? He changes his mind too late: the guilt would forever eat into his peace. Thus the worker, the student, and the middle class: all these elements experience forms of racism. Race is a significant political reality.

Every emigrant, individually and collectively, is thus involved in a shattering experience or other that alters his view of life, England and the world. Perhaps the biggest transformation is in Tornado who earlier, in the barber's shop, had seen the English people en masse as the enemy. In the crucible of experience and hardships, he matures into a more discriminating and accommodating vision. While rejecting the injustices and humiliations inevitable in a class and colour conscious society, he finds his solidarity with suffering humanity. Love, for him, now becomes a healing medicine. He says:

> I been getting' the feelin' lately that I ain't got no right to hate anybody, cause a man ain't nothin' in particular.

> Not even the English?

> Not even they . . . But even take the English. My feelin' for them was no hate, not real hate, 'cause when I come to think of it, if they'd just show one sign of friendship, just a little sign of appreciation for people like me an' you who from time we born, in school an' after school, we wus hearin' about them, if they would understan' that an' be different, then all the hate you talk 'bout would disappear.[36]

Imperialism is of course the root basis of racist hate and not the other way round. Universal human love is only possible through the end of imperialism and the class system that together generate racist oppression. What Tornado is driving at is that racism is not rooted in biology but in the social make up. What is social can be changed by the social intervention of human beings.

Nevertheless Tornado's tone pervades the novelistic resolution

---

[36] Ibid., p. 191.

of their harsh encounter with the reality behind the idea of England. In the 1983 Schocken edition of *In the Castle of My Skin*, Lamming, lamented the mildness of the resolution of the riot scene where the landlord is threatened but not physically molested. He tried to make a distinction between the realism of what is and that of what could be.

The novelist does not only explore what happened. At a deeper level of intention than literal accuracy, he seeks to construct a world that might have been; to show the possible as a felt and a living reality.[37]

The same comments could apply equally to *The Emigrants*. The intensity of the first section of the novel entitled 'The Voyage', when the emigrants are virtually driven by the idea of England almost like a political fatal attraction to the land of the enemy is not matched by that of the second section entitled 'Room and Residents' or the third, 'Another Time'. Something more should have happened to balance the intensity of the expectations of the first section. The mood in the second and third parts may be closer to the historical realism of the period, but not necessarily to the realism of the spirit of history. The racism these emigrants encounter was to generate, years later, in the eighties, the resistance that took the form of the Brixton race riots.

Water with Berries published in 1971 is almost a revisit of the second and third sections of *The Emigrants*. The three main artists, three versions of Caliban in reverse – call them three Calibans in Prospero's Country – could have been variations of Collis and other middle-class intellectuals of *The Emigrants*. Teeton, Roger and Derek choose England as the place of their exile because they are also conditioned by the same idea of England as an inheritance and a refuge. In this narrative there is more violence in the resolution of conflicts. Once again the conflicts have their origins in the colonial situation. For although San

---

[37] *In the Castle of My Skin*, pp. xiii-xiv.

Cristobal of their upbringing and the site of political struggle is now independent, it is only so in form. It is now under a more ruthless control of the finance capital of its northern neighbour. The ruling ethic is still one that makes peace with imperialism. The historical roots of that temperament lie in the colonial era of British imperialism which had shaped the minds of the class and had made them 'pupils to its language and its institutions.'[38] They are an extension of the overseer class described in *In the Castle of My Skin* as looking down upon the masses as 'low down nigger people' who stood in the way of progress. It is an overseer class which had been schooled into carrying the 'world of the others imagined perfection' like 'a dead weight upon their energy'. This class spoke of their own people as the enemy:

You never can tell with my people. It was the language of the Government servant, and later the language of lawyers and doctors who had returned stamped like an envelope with what they called the culture of the Mother Country.[39]

In the *Black World* interview Lamming states his belief that it was against all reason that colonialism as a history, which had held communities and peoples in so much oppressive violence, could come to an end in a cordial manner:

That horror and brutality have a price, which has to be paid by the man who inflicted it

– just as the man who suffered it has to find a way of exorcising that demon. It seems to me that there is almost therapeutic need for a certain kind of violence in the breaking. There cannot be a parting of the ways. There has to be a smashing.[40]

The acts of violence in *Water with Berries*, albeit at a personal level, are therefore meant as symbols of the 'end of a social

---

[38] Op. cit., p. xii.
[39] Ibid., p. 27.
[40] Op. cit., p. 91.

order that deserves to be destroyed.'[41]

This may explain the one problematic in *Water with Berries*: the fate of the women characters. Lamming is sensitive to gender oppressions as much as he is to those of race and class. But all the main women characters in *Water with Berries* end up dead or violated at the hands of the male. Roger, the musician, drives his white American wife, Nicole, to her death with his accusation that the child she carries is not his; what he really fears is the whiteness of the child she might bear, a reversal of Shakespeare's Prospero fearing the blackness of the children Caliban might have borne with Miranda. Derek, the actor, tries to rape the girl on the stage negating the role of the corpse that he had been relegated to playing. This is another replay of the Caliban's trying to 'rape' Miranda. And then there is Teeton's encounter with Miranda on Hampstead Heath through a symbolic ceremony of the Souls. In the mysterious encounter played entirely in the dark, Teeton learns that Miranda had been gang raped by the slaves on her father's plantation, that is Prospero's plantation, in San Cristobal. Teeton's wife, Randa, who is talked about in the narrative but never makes an appearance commits suicide. Seven years before, in San Cristobal, she had given herself to the American ambassador so that this representative of the powerful northern neighbour could intervene with the neocolonial regime to secure Teeton's release from prison and escape from an almost certain death because of his involvement in revolutionary politics. He cannot stand being eternally indebted to the representative of imperialism for his very existence. But in England he comes under the protection of the Old Dowager, a repeat of *Water with Berries*, for it turns out that she is no other than the resurrected Mrs Prospero. In the end, he kills her, to free himself from her subject in a neo-protectorate. Is Lamming romanticising the

---

[41] *In the Castle of My Skin,* p. xiv.

therapeutic effects of violence? When Fanon talks of violence as constituting the decolonisation process, he is basically talking about organised revolutionary violence and not necessarily the individual acts of violence. Lamming would share Fanon's revolutionary ends: to overturn the entire socio-economic whole. However Lamming works in Symbols. The novel, *Water with Berries*, as much as the earlier one, *The Emigrants*, is dealing with the colonially nurtured image of the colonising country, Prospero's country, as the mother, The Mother Country. The clue, to the symbolic intentions of the author of *Water with Berries*, then, lies in the name of the Old Dowager, Mrs Gore Brittain. Teeton is breaking the psychological contract with the coloniser's country. His independence is dependent on his cutting himself loose from the dependence complex implied in the colony accepting the coloniser's view of himself as the Mother.

The psychological 'contract' with the idea of the base of the colonial order so well dramatised in *The Emigrants*, gives clue to an understanding of neocolonialism as a phenomenon in history and world politics. Colonialism did not only make communities captives of foreign economies and politics but also psychic captives through cultural control. An aspect of that control is the obsession of the colonised with the image of the 'mother' country. The dwellers in the colony, at least the educated upper echelon, come to more than identify with the language and culture of their colonial inheritance. They become obsessed by it almost as if they are under the spell of a spiritual possession. Even the most progressive are not immune from this spirit possession by the image of the benevolent mother.

As recently as 1995 in *Jeune Afrique* the Congolese novelist, Henri Lopès, could write with glowing terms of endearment about francophonie and the French language. For him French has become a superafrican language despite the fact that even for his own country it is spoken by a minority only. He maintains that French is no longer a foreign language and that henceforth it is an African language. *'Le français n'est plus une langue étrangère. C'est desormais une langue africaine.'* He moves from the concept of Francophonie as a language to it as a social and political family. *'La francophonie c'est pour moi tout à la fois une langue, une famille et, peut-être, une politique.'*[42]

Lopès is following in the footsteps of Léopold Sédar Senghor. Senghor, even as President of Senegal, retained his French citizenship, and chose France as the place of his retirement. Bokassa of the Central African Republic recreated for his own coronation the symbols of a similar coronation of the Napoleonic era in France. C.L.R. James, in *The Black Jacobins*, explains the failure of Toussaint L'Ouverture in terms of that obsession with the 'mother' country: he could not conceive the future of Haiti without France. Aimé Césaire, the author of the brilliant *Discourse on Colonialism* and *Return to My Native Land*, the pathfinder of the radical line in Negritude that stretches from him to its progressive fruition in Fanon opposes the independence of Martinique from France. How does one explain this phenomenon except in Lamming's terms of minds stamped like envelopes with the culture of the mother country? It is the classic psychological cases of children's attachment to their mothers and refusing to be weaned of mother's milk.

In the name of the mother, the native ruling elite in the postcolonial era have made a cultural contract with the country of their coloniser. And once again Lamming, in 1954, before many countries in Asia and Africa and the Caribbean islands were independent, was able to capture its psychic hold on the colonised. His work as a whole, from *In the Castle of My Skin, The Emigrants, Of Age and Innocence* and *A Season of Adventure* to *Water with Berries* and *Natives of My Person,* is a grand epic of the decolonisation process. The deconstruction of the mother

---

[42] Henri Lopès, 'Francophonie: demain, peut-être', *Jeune Afrique,* no. 1822, 1995.

image is integral to his revolutionary aesthetics. His aesthetics are also dialectical. Breaking the mental contract with the coloniser's country is a necessary step in the liberation process. Complete economic and political decolonisation is not possible without cultural and psychological liberation. Equally true, psychological and cultural break with the mesmerising power and worship of the coloniser's language and culture is not possible without political and economic liberation. People can never be free without the liberation of the wholeness of their economy, politics and culture.

This explains why Lamming's work is an argument with Shakespeare. For Shakespeare became one of the prime symbols of British culture. Even the revolutionary aspect of Shakespeare's work which evoked sympathy and recognition in the colonial intellectual, was tamed and co-opted by the colonising classes: it was part of the package of Shakespeare as an icon of Western civilisation. Had any of the native cultures produced an epic, let alone a Shakespeare? Shakespeare the icon demonstrated the superiority of Western civilisation over native cultures particularly those which, though rich in orature, were without a written script. Lamming's work seems to be saying this: Shakespeare had a mother, yes; but so have all the Lammings of the world. Prospero had a mother language; so had Caliban. But it is possible for a Caliban to be so mesmerised by the claimed universality of Prospero's language as to forget that the claim was, and still is, an instrument of economic and political control. Caliban has to find his real connection with Sycorax, his mother, and her language, as a basis of his dialogue with all the sons and daughters of all the other mothers in the world.

Freeing the Imagination*
Lamming's Aesthetics
of Decolonisation

It was A.N. Whitehead who once said that Western philosophy was a 'series of footnotes to Plato'.[1] By this he did not mean that there was no originality in later Western philosophy but rather that many of the themes that came to dominate that tradition were anticipated in Plato's work. There is a way in which the same can be said of the literature of decolonisation in relation to Lamming's work, in particular his text *In the Castle of My Skin*, which in many ways anticipated the themes in Fanon's *Wretched of the Earth*; Albert Memmi's *The Colonizer and the Colonized* and other contemporary anti-colonial texts. Lamming's work that followed, *Of Age and Innocence; The Pleasures of Exile* and *Season of Adventure* were to elaborate on themes already touched in that seminal text of the aesthetics of decolonisation written by one just past his early twenties.

Even the date of its publication, 1954, marks a great moment in the praxis of decolonisation. It is a moment pregnant with the tension between what had been a century of European Imperial ascendancy in the globe with French and British Empires at the helm and what was about to be the redrawing of the power map

* Address at the conference on 'The Sovereignty of the Imagination; The Writings and Thought of George Lamming', University of the West Indies Mona campus, Kingston, Jamaica, 5-7 June 2003; first published in *Sovereignty of the Imagination* (Kingston: Arawak Publications 2004), and as Foreword for *The George Lamming Reader: The Aesthetics of Decolonisation* edited by Anthony Bogues (Kingston & Miami: Ian Randle Publishers 2011)
[1] Alfred North Whitehead, *Process and Reality* (Free Press, 1979, p. 39).

of the world by the forces of decolonisation. The redrawing had already started with India's independence in 1947; the Chinese Revolution in 1948; the defeat of the French in Indo-China at Dien Bien Phu in 1954; the start of the Mau Mau armed challenge to the British colonial state in Kenya in 1952; and a similar armed challenge against the French in Algeria. There was also Ghana's Independence in 1957; the Cuban revolution in 1956; the rise of the Civil Rights Movement in America marked by the now famous act of Rosa Parks refusing to give up her seat to a white person in Alabama; not to mention the workers' movements in Asia, Africa and the Caribbean often marked by general strikes and mass uprisings. In short, Lamming emerges at the high noon of anti-imperialism, the forcible entry of the masses into history. His work is simultaneously a product, a reflection and a celebration of a people making history.

The narrative structure of *In the Castle of My Skin* reflects that centrality of people in history. The community of ordinary men and women and children is the principle actor. Multiple voices are given equal space in the narrative. Their awakening from just a people in themselves, with lives governed by a mythic consciousness and local allegiance, to a people for themselves, governed by a vision that goes well beyond the boundaries of the village, the Caribbean shores to the outer arena of black and social struggles worldwide, is the central drama of the narrative.

Trumper's remarkable journey to America and back illustrates this. You will recall that Trumper is one of the group of youths with whom boy G, one of the narrative voices, grows up. We are told that after going to America, in the midst of the Civil Rights Movements, he comes back with an outlook that confuses the others while it also fascinates them. In America, among other things, Trumper has gone through experiences that make him understand the baritone voice of Paul Robeson singing *Let My People Go*. The concept of the people, my people, becomes the centre-piece of Trumper's new vision.[2] But who are my people, the other youths ask, for clearly Trumper is talking of a reality that embraces more than the village, more than Caribbean nationalism, more than race even. My People. In the tone with which Trumper repeats the vision, it is suggestive of Garvey's racial pride, Du Bois' social consciousness in *Souls of Black Folk*, and of the earlier Toussaint L'Ouverture, whose entry into history through mobilisation of the slaves as 'My People' is dramatised and celebrated in C.L.R. James' *Black Jacobins*, a text which Lamming himself discusses in *The Pleasures of Exile*, as *Caliban Orders History*.[3] He describes the book as a West Indian classic, and recommends it as bible reading.[4] That concept of 'My People' underlies James' analysis of both the rise and the fall of Toussaint L'Ouverture. After initial hesitation to join the revolt of the masses Toussaint, the liberator, is seen as connecting with people; while Toussaint, the fallen, has become so, through disconnecting with the people, a judgement that James renders on the hero of his narrative and which Lamming endorses in his summary of the classic.

What is this encapsulated in the phrase 'My People' to which even Trumper is not quite able to give words? I want to suggest that it is the concept of the subject becoming the sovereign, the sovereignty of the people. The notion of the sovereign, the one who, whether embodied in a person or a state, 'renders habitual obedience to no one' as opposed to the subject who 'renders habitual obedience to the sovereign'[5] is important in theories of the state and legal thought. And even the notion of sovereignty

---

[2] As a twenty-one year old, Lamming, who by then had left Barbados for Trinidad did attend a concert given by Paul Robeson on his only visit to Trinidad, at the Carib Theatre, about 1948. 'That was an extraordinary moment! It was one those holy moments,' Lamming describes the experience in an interview with David Scott, *Small Axe, a Caribbean Journal of Criticism*, September 2002.

[3] *The Pleasures of Exile* (London, 1960, p. 118).

[4] Ibid., p.119.

[5] H.L.A. Hart, *The Concept of Law* (Oxford 1961).

lying with the people is not unique or original to Lamming. It is in fact central to many European theories of the state and state power.

In Hobbes' *Leviathan*, the people, to escape the state of nature marked by 'warre of every one against every one', which of course makes their life 'solitary, poore, nasty, brutish, and short', surrender their sovereignty to the state and its ruler. Although Locke of the *Two Treatises of Government*, takes the opposite view, that the state of nature is not governed by *constant warfare and strife*, still he shares the view that people surrender their rights of self-rule to the state. Though the sovereign power remains with the people who have the right to recall or reclaim their rights by dispensing with the government officials and even dismantling pre-existing orders, and unlike the Hobbesian ruler from whom the surrendered sovereignty can never be recalled, they both share the common starting point of people first surrendering their agency to the safekeeping of the sovereign, resident in the state or a central political power.

Rousseau differs with the two because for him sovereignty, which began with the people, remains there: it cannot be represented, for the same reason that it cannot be alienated: an active citizenry was the central pillar of a well-functioning political system where the affairs of the political authority and the citizens are closely intertwined.

Rousseau's concept of the sovereignty of the people comes closest to Lamming's.

But while Rousseau's people are undifferentiated, Trumper's 'My People' hints of the working people in the Gramscian notion of subaltern or that assumed by Walter Rodney, in his histories of *How Europe Underdeveloped Africa* and *A History of Guyanese Working People*, the preface to the latter written by Lamming.

In Lamming sovereignty lies with the subject freed from his subjection to an oppressing other, free to regain his own subjectivity as an agent of his being. For to be subject to another, an oppressing other, be he a foreigner or a national, is to have one's capacity for imagining a different future limited. In a colonial context, this sovereignty is not yet realised, it is an ideal for which to struggle.

It is this concept of the people which underlies the totality of Lamming's sensibility from *In the Castle of My Skin* to *Natives of My Person*. It is the possibility of this people being organised, taking back their sovereignty, which terrifies the colonial state and the nascent middle class of the colonial stage of imperialism, and for whom, 'the enemy is My people. My people don't like to see their people get on. The language of the civil servant. The myth had eaten into their consciousness like moths through the pages of ageing documents'.[6] Nothing dramatises this terror better than the overseer of *In the Castle of My Skin* who sees this people as jealous and about to destroy his privileged position as recipient of the remnants from the colonial master's table. The overseer mutates into the entire slimy group whose historical mission and destiny is that of replacing the colonial settler. Trumper comes back with the greatest contempt for this group which he sees as being in league with the Creightons of the colonial world. In short, the settler/colonial state may depart through the front door but it leaves behind its representatives in the newly independent estate, what Lamming used to call the caretaker government in both the sense of acting on behalf of imperial interests and also its short-lived, temporary character. Thus in *In the Castle of My Skin*, Lamming anticipated the betrayal of Independence, a theme he takes up in *Season of Adventure*, narrative that dramatises neocolonialism long before it had been part of common political parlance. The Slimies of the colonial world have taken over power and what they reproduce is a mimicry of the mother country.

[6] *In the Castle of My Skin* (Ann Arbor Paperbacks, 1991, pp. 26-7).

This slimy class is tied with cultural umbilical cords to the culture of the mother country through education as mutilation of memory or else as production of amnesia about a people's history. It is, once again, in *In the Castle of My Skin* where mutilation and amnesia are dramatised. One of the most memorable scenes is where the school kids are discussing slavery as something which belongs to a myth in a distant past. Slavery has nothing to do with them, it happened to others. The school reproduces the notion of Barbados as Little England, a replica of Big England. This is more real for it is played over and over again in the colonial narrative in books and on the blackboard. In *Season of Adventure*, the narrator stops the narrative to describe his relationship to Powell about to face murder. It is the school that differentiates their two fates; one accessed the school; the other did not, but, according to the narrative, he still bears responsibility for his brother's fate. He accepts responsibility but how many of the middle-class inheritors of Independence accept the responsibility of mass poverty and degradation?

In the colonial and even the post-independence school, language plays a crucial role in producing and reproducing cultural dependency on the mother country, for language is the rubber stamp that certifies that the neocolonial mind is truly made in Europe. In all his works, both creative and critical, Lamming comes back to the issue of education, culture and language. The two icons of this system are English and Shakespeare. They are also the greatest exports of the Empire. Note that in themselves there is nothing wrong but only how they are used. The colonised has never, can never produce Shakespeare. And Caliban has no language. He can only be taught and given language.

Prospero keeps on reminding Caliban of his debt to Prospero's language and culture. You did not know yourself until I gave you language. I created you but, of course, in my image. We encounter the phenomenon in Defoe's *Robinson Crusoe* where

Crusoe is teaching Friday language. Your name is Friday. My name is Master. Language here is being used to reproduce a master and slave consciousness to reinforce the material reality of the same. If Friday or his earlier manifestation in Caliban were to accept that language as used by the master, then he would enter a permanent state of auto-enslavement, surrendering his own sovereignty for ever.

That is why Lamming's work as a whole is a continuous argument with Shakespeare and English. He must deconstruct the two icons to reveal the way they have been used as an enslaving aesthetic in order to construct the foundation of a liberating aesthetic reflecting a sovereign people whose capacity to imagine a new world, whole, unfragmented, is set free. This would be a people who have overcome a state of alienation imposed on others.

For colonialism, as it emerges in Lamming's work, is indeed a system of alienation. It turns a people's land, labour, power, values, psyche even, into an enemy, a threat as in the case of the Overseer. Colonialism is a totality of alienation and when this is later nationalised into a norm in the postcolonial state it becomes the most dangerous threat to our imagination of a different sovereignty.

Lamming's project is an interrogation of the colonial process seen as integral to a capitalist modernity now mutating as globalisation with a global slime in power subjecting the globe to its narrow view of what it is to be human. This interrogation is a necessary step in the decolonisation of the economy, the politics, the culture and the psyche of the formerly colonised and now still dominated.

Central to the concept of the people, is labour, as a moulder of nurture. The highest representative of labour is the artist, for labour itself is seen as having the power to transform. The artist, seen as belonging to the category that Lamming often describes as cultural workers, draws from the imagination as his primary means of production. Imagination is the supreme sovereign for it is not bound by time and space and authority. No authority can enforce a command: Don't imagine. Don't dream. In that sense even within an oppressive system the artist can still exercise the sovereignty of his imagination to dream of new worlds. The artist and the worker are allies in the quest for freedom.

A constant image in his work is the ceremony of Souls. The invocation of the ceremony is like an artistic process that connects and heals. Lamming's own literary project is truly a huge artistic strife for the recovery of memory and the resurrection of the mutilated. The totality of his work is itself then a ceremony of resurrection, the recovery of our right to imagine, and it belongs to Caribbean, African, Asian and European peoples, indeed to all the social forces seeking unity to create a world reflective of human need not greed. His work is a site of the aesthetic of resistance and human liberation. He has built an artistic house for MY PEOPLE and I am so thrilled to be part of this event that pays tribute to his genius.

Nation in the Underground
Alex la Guma's
In the Fog of the Seasons' End

Alex la Guma *A Walk in the Night* (Ibadan: Mbari 1962; London: Heinemann 1967; AWS 35 1967)

—— *In the Fog of the Seasons' End* (London: Heinemann 1972; AWS 110 1972; New York: Third Press 1973)

—— *Time of the Butcherbird* (London: Heinemann 1979; AWS 212)

Alex la Guma, like Luandino Vieira, is an example of the writer in politics in both his life and works. A trade union organiser, a member of the South African Communist Party and ANC, he died in Cuba as the ANC ambassador in Havana. He was among the 156 in the notorious Treason Trial of 1956 and in later years he was placed under house arrest before being forced into exile in 1966. In his works from *A Walk in the Night* (1962) to *Time of the Butcherbird* (1979) he explores the interactions of race and class in both domination and resistance in South Africa. He is interested in capturing the life as lived by the urban worker and other social strata in South Africa. The inner life of the characters is rooted in palpable social conditions. The social milieu he describes is not pretty: it is one of greed on one hand and degradation on the other. His characters live in three spheres which are part of each other: the private, the domestic and the public. The private sphere is the realm of the inner dreams, frustrations, hopes, pain, memories of grief and loss as well as moments of happiness. The domestic is the realm of family life, its absence and presence, its tensions and tenderness, its promises and failures, its possibilities in a different South Africa. Both the private and the domestic are conditioned by the public sphere of work in industry and in government and by the operations of power in South African society. The public sphere in this case includes the police stations, prisons, law courts, and other institutions of life in apartheid South Africa. All these spheres bear indelible marks of race and class struggles. Despite the pain of loss and torture, the most abiding emotion in his works is that of hope. There will be a tomorrow. Dawn is on the horizon. The links of numerous acts of resistance by ordinary folk as they go about their business will be victorious. More so if they are organised. This is most visibly apparent in his novel, *In the Fog of the Seasons' End*. The very title bespeaks of this hope. What we see in the South Africa of the time of the writing, the all pervasive terrifying power of apartheid, was only the fog that comes at a season's end or the darkness before dawn. But this dawn will not come of itself. It will be the result of social and political struggles. La Guma has faith in the organised power of the black worker in South Africa and that is why he is so confident of the coming dawn. The legal liberation movements may be banned, exiled, and its leadership imprisoned or killed, but there is life underground. And this is one of the major themes in this political novel. It is a narrative of life underground, its fears, tensions, dangers, terror, its cowardice, courage, heroism, its moments of defeats and victory. But at the end of it all are the glimpses of the dawn of the liberation of South Africa. There is much optimism in this narrative but it is an optimism completely rooted in realism.

The novel opens with the arrest of Elias Tekwane, alias Hazel, and the beginnings of his interrogation at the torture chambers of the South African police, which will lead to his death towards the end of the narrative. Like Domingos Xavier in Vieira's novel, he does not tell the secrets of the organisation. The novel then turns to the near-the-end of the action. What we get thereafter is a tracing back of the events leading to the last but fatal meeting between Beukes and Tekwane. Tekwane, the older, the more experienced is caught and Beukes, the younger, escapes, wounded, but he will complete the mission. The torch has been passed on to the younger generation. But in another sense the narrative does open with the opening, because the real opening of any narrative of South African life under apartheid is violence. Apartheid itself is a system of violence. The action of the novel moves through this landscape of violence in time and space. And both movements, in time through Tekwane, and in space through Beukes, are stalked with state terrorism and people's resistance. The space is in the present. But it is the same space that Tekwane had traversed many times before his present arrest. Elias Tekwane is Beukes in history and Beukes is Elias Tekwane in the present and in the future. Tekwane may die but he lives in the thousands of young men and women who have received his message through Beukes and gone abroad for training to come back and wage the armed struggle as part of a continuum.

It is Beukes who walks us through the social landscape in space. He is part of an underground organisation and makes various rendezvous and unplanned encounters which culminate in some of the young recruits of the unnamed political organisation escaping abroad to train in armed warfare. Miss Adams is one of those unplanned encounters but she is part of the social landscape. As a nanny to white children, she exemplifies the irony of apartheid South Africa. White children are brought up by black mothers and when they grow up, they become part of the system and turn against them. Miss Adams recognises this but accepts it as a fact of life: 'What can us people do?' she asks (*In the Fog of the Seasons' End*, p. 11). To Beukes' assurance that there were things that people could do, she answers back with pessimism: 'it's so hopeless. You only get into trouble.' But her position is slightly more honest than that of the Bennet family who have a rendezvous with Beukes but when he turns up are not at home. By their action, by not doing their part in the chain of actions and contacts, they can easily undermine the entire enterprise. Confronted by Beukes with his betrayal, Bennet can only prevaricate, become evasive, try to blame it all on his wife and then offer money as part of his contribution. The Bennets are some of the up-and-coming petty bourgeoisie with a decent house which they fear to lose through visible involvement in the struggle. But their hold on property is precarious anyway, because as blacks or coloureds, nonwhites, they can be removed from the residential areas anytime, as historically happened in Sophiatown, a fate documented in Bloke Modisane's *Blame Me on History*[11] and in Miriam Tlali's *Muriel at the Metropolitan*.[22] Not surprisingly, Beukes rejects the money, telling Bennet (a half-hearted chequebook revolutionary) that he didn't have to buy his way out of the struggle.

La Guma comments through juxtaposition of situations and characters. Thus both Miss Adams' position and Bennet's are immediately contrasted with those of the next encounters. The taxi driver for instance is in the same kind of social class as Miss Adams. But he is more outspoken against the system. His question to Beukes ('reckon that we shall win?') carries more optimism than Miss Adams' noncommittal fatalism or Bennet's prevarications. Tommy, the other encounter, is lost in a world of cheap music from the West, or rather music acts as some kind of drug into which he escapes so as not to know fully the realities of the present. But he does things, even risky things, for the

---

[1] Bloke Modisane *Blame Me on History* (New York: Simon and Schuster, 1990).

[2] Miriam Tlali *Muriel at the Metropolitan: A Novel* (London: Longman, 1979) and *Between Two Worlds* (Peterborough ONT: Broadview Press, 2004). The memory of the destruction of Sophiatown is a formative factor in Muriel's political consciousness.

movement out of friendship and personal loyalty to Beukes. Mr Flotman, the school teacher is in a similar class position to Bennet, but he risks his job, whatever it is worth, to take handbills to have them distributed by some of the school children. The penalty for urging the armed overthrow of the apartheid regime is death. So he is taking genuine risks as also do the school children. His actions once again are part of a larger chain. It is through him that the narrative makes a critique of an education system that aims to inculcate in the minds of blacks that white rule in South Africa is through divine right. Abdalla is a factory worker, used to organising, to the idea of strikes, to being at the forefront. He is critical of some of the union leaders who have become just a little bourgeois in their outlook on the organisation of confrontation. Abdalla takes the political leaflets for distribution in the factory. He is moved not only by what he sees as part of the workers' daily life under apartheid but also by the memories of the past injustices, like when workers were killed during what he calls the big strike that resulted in the Sharpeville massacre:

> How can it be that they just shoot people just because they come and say, 'Look we're not slaves, we only want our rights?' Just to give the order to shoot, just like that. Look we are all humans, don't I say? (p. 96)

He is a Muslim and without the narrator saying so directly, it shows that people of different religious faiths can be found on both sides of the struggle, some with the regime and others against it depending on their class position and degree of politicisation. There is also the doctor to whose clinic Beukes runs for treatment. He is probably a white doctor in a much more privileged position but he is clearly a fellow traveller with the underground movement. At least he does treat those on the run. And it is through him that the narrative articulates arguments about the morality of the law. He explains why he breaks the law by treating those who are defying the law:

> If the community is given the opportunity of participating in making the law, then they have a moral obligation to obey it. But if the law is made for them, without their consent or participation, then it is a different matter. However even under the circumstances prevailing in our country, I must ask myself, what does this law or that law defend, even if I did not help to make it? If the law punishes a crime, murder, rape, then I could bring myself to assist it. But if the law defends injustice, prosecutes and persecutes those who fight against injustice, then I am under no obligation to uphold it. (p.161)

Finally there are all the youth, with their *nom-de-guerres*, who are risking their lives by going abroad to train for the armed struggle. These represent continuity and the future and are the culmination of the territorial and historical landscape. They represent the various types in the South African struggle in the present as well as being a part of all those who had been there before them, such as Elias Tekwane.

Elias Tekwane through whom the social landscape in time is seen is actually 40 years of age although his papers claim that he is about 50. Where Beukes is urban born and is coloured in the South African racial classification, Tekwane is a black African, a veteran of the struggle and born in the countryside. He never met his father, a miner, who died in a mining accident in Johannesburg. His mother is cheated out of the meagre pension whereas the wives of the white victims are pensioned for life. He starts to work early, first as a sweeper in a Mr Wiseman's shop. As a youth he had heard about the Anglo-Boer war and the First World War. When the Second World War comes, he volunteers to fight against the Hitler regime when some of the whites were yearning to fight on the side of the Nazis. But he is too young and even then he is chastised by his employer for so volunteering. How dare he, a black native, get involved in the

affairs of the whites? Nevertheless the advent of the Second
World War brings new openings. There is labour shortage
during the war and Tekwane signs up for work in the city. To do
this he has to get a passbook. La Guma uses this to introduce
the politics of race and identity symbolised by the pass system.
The whole question is summed up in the authorial voice of the
omniscient narrator:

> When African people turn to sixteen they are born again or, even
> worse, they are accepted into the mysteries of the Devil's mass,
> confirmed into the blood rites of a servitude as cruel as Caligula,
> as merciless as Nero. Its bonds are the entangled chains of infinite
> regulations, its rivets are driven in with rubber stamps, and the
> scratchy pens in the offices of the Native Commissioners are like
> branding irons which leave scars for life. (p. 80)

The entire symbolism is in religious terms. With the pass in
one's hands, one had the 'permission to exist as shown by the
fact that you have registered with the authorities; and to leave
the place of your previous existence; permission to arrive in *this*
place by the grace of God and the Native commissioner'. Thus
Tekwane and his life are used to sum up the reality of life for the
non-white in apartheid South Africa. He is also used to sum up
the development of the political struggle, particularly after the
Second World War. As a worker in the towns he joins in strikes.
One of the biggest strikes resulted in the Sharpeville massacre,
a defining moment in the national liberation struggle. Prisons
become political schools or rather recruitment centres; and it is
from such a prison that Tekwane is introduced into the movement
in which he becomes a dedicated and active member. When the
liberation movement goes underground, Tekwane becomes one
of the regional organisers. It is in fact as an organiser of the
underground that he first meets Beukes. Their meeting and work
together symbolise the coming together of the black and those

defined as coloureds and brings together the urban and rural sensibility as well as the experience of the seasoned hand and the youth ready to take up the torch to light the way for tomorrow.

La Guma does not romanticise the life underground. Its success depends so much on a chain of trust and faith and one could never be sure of either. With the banning of legal overt organisations, regrouping becomes difficult. The liberation movement after the ban is compared to 'a slugged boxer, shaking his spinning head to clear it, while he took count, waiting to rise up before the final ten' (p. 48). Most of the leaders and the cadres were then in prisons or in exile, whilst behind them, all over the country, tiny groups and individuals who had escaped the net still moved like moles underground, trying to link up in the darkness of lost communications and broken contacts. 'Some of them knew each other and wrestled to patch up the body. They trusted each other because without trust, they were useless. They burrowed underground, changing their nests and lairs frequently' (p. 48).

Discipline and secrecy were necessary to ensure security of the organisation. But how can anyone be sure when there are obviously many weak links in the chain of organised human contacts? The weakness could manifest itself in different ways: like the Bennets being wedded more to the 'brass ornaments and polished furniture' of their house than they are to the movement. Or Tommy who is lost in the world of cheap music and does things only out of personal loyalties. Faith and trust were necessary but faith also depended on mistrust, being on one's guard all the time. Waiting for Beukes at their rendezvous, Tekwane muses over the precariousness of the situation. Beukes had inspired faith in him

> but these days one could not depend only on faith: the apparatus of
> the Security Police scraped away faith and perseverance like strata

of soil until they came to what was below. It was the hard granite on which they floundered. (p.131)

Workers in the underground have almost no real domestic life, which is often lived in memories like Beukes' constant thoughts of the hearth and his wife Frances and their child. The longing for a life of domestic ease could itself be a weakness but it could also be a strength. There can never be domestic tranquility in a situation where to quote Fanon, 'the police are the harbinger of violence in every home'. In the case of apartheid South Africa there is absolutely no possibility of any domestic sphere for the many who have to leave their villages and work in the mines where family life is literally banned.

There are also no larger than life heroics in the characters of the narrative. The characters are ordinary people, workers, taxi drivers, the unemployed, and they live in terror. And yet heroism comes from that very consciousness of danger, from the knowledge that danger lurks somewhere in a corner, and that betrayal and accidents were always possible. In La Guma's world, characters and actors are at their most vulnerable in their moments of greatest confidence. Heroism for La Guma lies precisely in the consciousness of the difficulties, the dangers, the acknowledgement of the fear within, and yet going about to do what has to be done, what is necessary for the movement and the welfare of others. Heroism lies in the ordinary acts of ordinary men and women driven by the need and the commitment to change intolerable social conditions. It consists in doing one's part in the link of chain of human struggle. The achievement, whatever it is, is not the result of the heroic activity of one individual but the results of the work of many hands and minds. Hence the successful mission of sending Paul, Peter, Henny April, Isaac for training in armed struggle is the result of all the characters inhabiting the social landscape of South Africa in time and place. It is because of the actions of Tekwane and others before him; it is because of the actions of Beukes and all the young men and women determined to see the struggle through the fog to see the seasons' end.

This raises the question of women's participation in the struggle. In this narrative, they are not seen at the forefront. They live as memories in the minds of the male actors. Tekwane remembers his mother and we know all about Frances, Beukes' wife, through his memories of her. Bennet's wife is always nagging and therefore adding to Bennet's anxiety. Were there no women underground cadres? White women are treated no better. They appear simply as appendages to a basically white male performance of terror. In the portrayal of white policemen and whites generally, La Guma differentiates between the small and the bigger fish. The policemen are a torture yes, but they also emerge as products or agents of a more sinister system of apartheid and imperialism. Women are caught up in the system too. But were there no white women perpetrators of the crimes of apartheid?

These questions must have occurred to La Guma because in the next novel, *Time of the Butcherbird*, published in 1979 there are in fact very strong women who are active on both sides of the struggle. Mma Tau, exiled in the country, continues with her agitation, opposing her brother, a traditional chief, when he prevaricates. She is the driving force behind the mobilisation and the awakening of the people in the countryside and she is very clear about collecting collective debts, in other words organised struggle, as opposed to the likes of Shilling Murile, who sees the struggle in personal terms of vengeance. Mma Tau is also the one who articulates the notion of the country joining hands with the cities to overthrow the system. She is talking of the worker peasant alliance. In its setting in the country and in its concerns with the theme of land, *Time of the Butcherbird*, and *In the Fog of the Seasons' End*, make a complementary political whole.

In the Fog of the Seasons' End was published in 1972, four years before the Soweto children's uprising against the apartheid education system and the subsequent massacres. *Time of the Butcherbird* was published in 1979 when the struggle had started to intensify following the Soweto uprisings. In the twenty years or so following the publication of *In the Fog*, the guerrilla warfare waged by the ANC cadres, the internal democratic agitation and international pressure, were all to intensify, forcing South Africa to change directions. ANC and all the other banned political organisations were legalised, Mandela and the other political prisoners were released, and South Africa was finally moving towards those outcomes hoped for and predicted by Alex la Guma in his writings particularly *In the Fog of the Seasons' End*.

'*La poésie veut quelque chose d'énorme, de barbare et de sauvage,*' once wrote Denis Diderot in *Oeuvres de théâtre de M. Diderot, avec un discours sur la poésie dramatique*, and certainly savage, barbaric apartheid oppression did ignite the poetic muse of many a South African writer, and turned Alex la Guma into one of the leading writers in politics in Africa. His work transcends historical apartheid and becomes part of the poetics of struggle and the affirmation of the human yearning for freedom.

Dialectics of Hope
Sembene's *God's Bits of Wood*

Sembene Ousmane *God's Bits of Wood* (Translated from the French by Francis Price; New York: Doubleday 1962; London: Heinemann AWS 63 1969; New York: Doubleday/Anchor 1971)

—— *Les bouts de bois de dieu; Banty Yam Mall* (Paris: Le Livre Contemporain 1960; Paris: Presses Pocket 1971)

Dialectical materialism which denotes that matter is the mother of social consciousness; that movement and change are the results of the collision of opposites; and hence the primacy of social struggle in changes in human society, is key to a fuller understanding of Sembene's work for dialectics is basic to his outlook. For him, social progress is the result of the mutual impact of phenomena; nurture out of nature; new out of the old; freedom out of confinement; thought and knowledge out of acts. He applies this dialectical outlook to history, in particular to colonialism and the struggles against it, struggles that produce a third reality, liberation as part of the overall quest for social justice and human freedom. The dialectical outlook and method inform all his work including the cinema but his use of dialectics is best seen in *God's Bits of Wood*.

God's Bits of Wood is about the awakening of African workers from a state of being a class in itself, to a state of class for itself within the overall context of the many-sided character of the anti-colonial struggle. Of particular interest is the development of a class based anti-colonial struggle that engulfs the whole of what was then French West Africa. Historically, this struggle was to lead to the fragmented independence of what later became Burkina Faso, Mali and Senegal. Sembene Ousmane has done a remarkable job in dramatising the workers' centrality in it. The movement from 'in-itself' to 'for-itself' can be seen in the growth and development of a critical consciousness among the workers as a result and in the course of their mass involvement in the strike. The word 'development' is appropriate because what is so remarkable about the novel is its dramatisation of the process of change, not as a mechanical progression from one state to another, but as a dialectical lurching forward, with events acting on each other, generating contradictions between whites and blacks, employers and workers, adults and children, men and women, old and the new, mind and body, humans and machinery. Development is born of the process of overcoming those contradictions, the partial or full solution of which takes society a step forward; but the new step may well be the site of new contradictions. Underlying the entire action of the novel is the assumption that change through struggle is inherent in nature, society, and thought. Asking questions about the unsatisfactory aspects of one's environment is the beginning of knowledge. And knowledge empowers the desire and the struggle for change. The struggle for change brings about new knowledge. A new more critical awareness of one's environment is an important measure of human development.

Not surprisingly one of the themes highlighted early on in the story is that of education, learning and knowledge. The theme is launched by the debate between Ad'jibid'ji, and her grandmother, Old Niakoro. In the initial stages, the women stay at home while the men go to the Union Building to discuss plans for a strike. The women do their traditional chores, not unduly concerned with what is happening out there. It is this gender division of roles that is challenged by Ad'jibid'ji's desire to know, a desire that leads her to the Union Building where crucial issues are being debated. To Old Niakoro, these are affairs of male adults. Even the quest for knowledge was a matter for men. Thus she is hurt that a girl should be interfering with matters that properly belong to males, and secondly, to adults. Although what makes Old Niakoro explode in anger is the fact that Ad'jibid'ji has used a French word, what really upsets her is that a little girl is answering back to an adult! Age and manhood as the traditional keepers of knowledge are being challenged by the actions of a girl-child through her actions and questions. The education she had received from her petit père, the narrative voice tells us, had made Ad'jibid'ji a precocious child, and it is this that leads her to question actions based on assumptions that cannot bear the light of reason. For instance, she had learned very quickly to make a distinction among punishments. So when Assitan, her mother, is about to punish her without first finding out what had really occurred between Niakoro and Ad'jibid'ji – it is enough that the grandmother is upset – Ad'jibid'ji asks her mother: 'was it to hurt her or to make her better?' When, in another conversation Fa Keïta asks why she goes to meetings held by men she says that she goes there to learn what it is to be a man, for woman and man will be equal one day.

Niakoro's position, in contrast to Ad'jibid'ji's, assumes that education and learning are an unquestioning acceptance of tradition. Education is no more than an inheritance of how and what has always been. Don't you believe that these children are making a mistake? She later asks Fa Keïta, in relation to the plans for the impending workers' strike. How could he, a wise man, listen to the words of infants? Fa Keïta replies that even the old must learn, and recognise that the things people know today were not born with them. Knowledge was not a hereditary thing. In response to Niakoro's appeal to the sanctity of white hairs, Fa

Keïta cautions her not to confuse respect with knowledge and cites the proverb that says before one has white hairs, one had to first have them black.

Here is a clear dramatisation of two types of education and learning: education as the development and reinforcement of critical consciousness contrasted with the concept of education as inheritance of tradition. The latter can at times provide a coherent and fairly consistent basis for making judgements on the present. For instance it makes Old Niakoro see that foreign languages can be oppressive; but that is only true in structures of foreign domination, in this case, the colonial context. This and her ready acceptance of traditional roles for women and children in society will be questioned by the reality and needs of the present struggle and historical moment and lead her to take actions that contribute to change even though she dies in the process.

Both learning as acceptance of the past and education as inculcation of a critical consciousness are next contrasted with education as a process of alienation from one's environment. Colonial education is precisely such a process and its effects are best seen in N'Deye Touti.

Having been to a teacher training school, N'Deye is the pretty public scribe for the whole neighborhood. But in reality she lives in a kind of separate world. The narrative voice tells us that the reading she did and the films she saw made her part of a universe in which her own people had no place and by the same token she no longer had a place in theirs. She dreams of a prince charming from the pages of a Mills and Boon type of literature where love was costume balls, yachting trips, vacations abroad, elegant anniversary presents and glossy automobiles:

> Real life was there; not here, in this wretched corner, where she was daily confronted with beggars and cripples at every turning. When N'Deye came out of a theatre where she had seen visions of mountain chalets deep in snow, of beaches where the great of

the world lay in the sun, of cities where the nights flashed with many-coloured lights, and walked from this world back into her own, she would be seized with a kind of nausea, a mixture of rage and shame. (p. 84)

In her own people she can only see what she calls lack of civilization. A film showing pygmies fills her with shame but another showing the ruins of ancient Greece fills her with the pride and wonder of an inheritor of a great past. She prides herself in knowing far more about Europe than she does about Africa. She had never read a book by an African author, quite sure that they could teach her nothing. She has no faith in the people and in their capacity to change anything. Common to all the French-language-speaking types like N'Deye is that they are products of the formal colonial school system.

Ad'jibid'ji, on the other hand, gets her main education from her interaction with the people in the public sphere. She is already beginning to selectively reject and accept certain aspects of both the past and the present. She knows Bambara, her language, very well, she is not ashamed of speaking it, but she is also studying French. She rejects the traditional role model of the submissive woman, but the rejection of her grandmother's and mother's image of the good woman as the one who knows her place, does not make her embrace the role model of the formally educated N'Deye Touti. In absorbing the new, appropriating the world of books, interacting with the public sphere, she is rooted in the positive elements of her culture like the respect she has for the elders!

In short, education for a critical consciousness is contrasted with the education – whether traditional or colonial – that gives the recipient a passive consciousness. And the formal schooling system is contrasted with the universities of the streets of social struggle. A characteristic of the universities of social struggle is its transforming effects on the recipients. One gets educated precisely in the very attempts to change a negative social environment. More important, one is transformed by that act of trying to transform. This in turn generates a more heightened consciousness, making the mind open and reach out for more. The strike in which the workers are now involved is an example of the transforming power of the universities of the streets of social struggle.

The strike is like a school for all of us, says Tiémoko before the trial of the ticket collector, Diara. Tiémoko, in fact, is a good example of this transforming effect. The first time we meet him, he is described in terms of his physique, his body. He is described as having a brutish head, 'a thirty-year old colossus with a thick-muscled body, enormous shoulders, and a bull neck' (p. 21) on which the veins pulse angrily. He is a mere body. It is revealed that at Bakayoko's urging Tiémoko had done a lot of reading without always understanding what he had read. And now in the absence of Bakayoko, and with the demands of the occasion, he is the one who comes up with the idea of a public people's trial of the offending Diara, Tiémoko's relative, and his trial is intended as an example to others. Tiémoko remembers one of the books he had read, Malraux's *La Condition Humaine*, and he goes for it to help him clarify some of the ideas germinating in his head. He leads the case for the prosecution and in this courtroom drama played out in the open, we, the readers, become witnesses to the integration of the body and the mind. Where before it was his muscles that were emphasised, here, now, it is what is in his head. Or rather, we see the dramatisation of Tiémoko's discovery of his mind, his intellect. He is very excited when the workers agree with his idea. Something is happening to him, something which had been buried by colonial capitalism, is being born. Colonial capitalism had seen in him only a body, muscles to engage the machine, brute force against mechanical force. Now he is a body that both works and thinks and it is this self-discovery that most excites him after his idea had prevailed: For the first time in his life, an idea of his was going to play a part in the lives of thousands of others. The narrating voice comments that it was not pride or vanity Tiémoko was experiencing, but the astonishing discovery of his worth as a human being.

But the transforming effect of the education in the school of social struggles is best seen in women. Sembene Ousmane, in this novel, is obviously critical of the status of women in society. Her traditional role, as defined by Niakoro in her arguments with Ad'jibid'ji, is for the woman to know her place in relation to the man. In Assitan, Ad'jibid'ji's mother, is a portrait of such a woman. Assitan had been married to Bakayoko's brother without being consulted over the matter. When he died during a previous strike years back, she was turned over to Ibrahim Bakayoko – again without any consultation about her feelings. She did as the custom decreed. She acted out the tradition of conditioned wifeliness: docile, submissive, and hard working, never speaking one word louder than another, giving no appearance of knowing anything whatsoever of her husband's activities.

Most of the women, at the beginning of the narrative, would more or less fit into that description. Soon they begin to play a role in the strike. At first the men are hardly aware of the women's involvement. But as the strike continues and the women become the sole bread winners in the family, the men begin to understand that just as the times were bringing forth a new breed of men, they were also bringing forth a new breed of women. In the course of the narrative, or rather, the strike, all the women are changed in one form or another. This is particularly sharply dramatised in the case of Ramatoulaye and Penda.

Ramatoulaye is a grandmother, an old woman, well respected in the community in Bamako; she is described as a 'walking encyclopedia of every family in the district'. She is the very embodiment of communal values. Her involvement in the strike begins simply as a search for food for the children. She becomes withdrawn, almost stern, her responsibilities having become great 'because the house of which she was the eldest was large: there were no less than twenty of "God's bits of wood"' (p. 40). But initially her concern is with the feeding of those twenty mouths. She is not unduly concerned with the strike, that was certainly an affair of men. And colonialism? That was too remote a concept to have anything to do with the immediate task of feeding her children.

Her first confrontation is with Hadramé. The shopkeeper refuses to let her have rice on credit. He fears the retribution from the colonialists who have told them not give supplies to the workers so that they can be starved into submission. But Ramatoulaye is shocked to see that neighbourliness, one of the most important communal values, does not count. Instead of giving her what she wants, he is actually urging her to bring the pressure on the men to go back to work. Yet in her very presence he is able to find rice for her brother, Mabigué, the wealthy chief of the district. It is not difficult for her to see and conclude and even tell Hadramé to his face that he and Mabigué are on the side of the colonialists.

The truth of this observation is reinforced in her next confrontation with El Hadji Mabigué. He too refuses to share anything with her and instead, with a pro-colonial religious homily, he urges her to pressure the men to stop resisting the will of God and go back to work. Arguing that God, after all, has assigned a rank, a place, and a certain role to every man, it was blasphemous to think of changing His design, including colonialism itself.

These two confrontations during which she threatens to fight back is the beginning of her real education. She tries to sort things out in her mind for she is beginning to see that the strike is not simply a dispute between the Worker and the Employer but rather that it is central to the colonial system. 'I don't know about the strike', she says to herself on her way from her brother's place, '…but the thing is that it gives us too much to think about' (p.69). But her mental awakening cannot be stopped now.

It is important to stress that her awakening is born of the struggle. This is symbolised by the fight with her brother's ram after it has come to her compound and eaten up the few grains of rice left for her 'God's Bits of Wood'. That whole struggle to kill the overfed is described in fairly minute details. They create a picture of transfiguration. Everybody is astonished by her newfound strength. How could she, who was so frail with age, find so much strength to fight back without fear of death? To which she replies that in the cruel times they were living through they must find their own strength.

This presages the coming battle between the women and the police after which, once again, the women emerge with even greater awakening, making them question things that go well beyond the immediate economic struggle of the workers. They even begin to question the colonial legal system. And here the education they have gained from the school of social struggle is contrasted with that which N'Deye, their would-be teacher, has gained from the colonial school system.

N'Deye had not taken part in the collective fight against the police who had come to arrest Ramatoulaye and she disapproves strongly of what the women have done. Why? Because she had learned at school about the workings of the law, and she had been taught that no one had the right to take the law in his own hands. In response to that position, the women begin to debate issues of law and justice. What was the relationship? N'Deye is arguing, more or less, that Ramatouyale should have been left to face the police alone. Now the police will surely come back for them all. Why? Ask the other women! Because they attacked the police while they were doing their duty. That's an offence against the law. And to the women's question about Mabigué's ram eating much-needed rice, she argues that they should have put a complaint against him with the police.

A brilliant restatement of the colonial law, and it is not surprising that the women whose minds have been awakened by the experience of the struggle now begin to question the authority and truth of her scholarship. Their position is best articulated by Mame Sofi who had never been to a formal school. She opposes the idea of Ramatoulaye cooperating with the police and says that N'Deye Touti, in spite of all her learning, is mistaken. What the women are raising by their actions are the more basic questions about justice and the actual interests served by the colonial legal system. But it is interesting that at this stage, Ramatoulaye, although disagreeing with N'Deye Touti, has no words with which to answer back. After all, so she reasons within, N'Deye Touti had studied and learned at the great school. She therefore compromises and accepts the individual responsibility advocated by N'Deye as opposed to the collective responsibility advocated by Mame Sofi. If the police come back she would cooperate with them in her own arrest. And so, without knowing it, N'Deye has successfully articulated the position of a prosecution witness for the colonial legal system.

The women's next important stage in their journey of individual and collective awakening is their confrontation with religious authority. Old Imam, Sérigne N'Dakarou, appeals to the women to disperse. Like Mabigué, he claims that God himself had decided that people should live side by side with colonialists 'and the French are teaching us how to make things we have not known and showing us how to make things that we need. It is not up to us to rebel against the will of God, even when the reasons for that will are a mystery to us' (p.124). Once again the rejection of both the reactionary religious authority and the sanctity of colonial laws is best symbolised by Ramatoulaye herself.

The Imam has come to the police station to persuade

Ramatoulaye to apologise to her brother Mabigué. The policemen of the soul and the actual policemen of the body combine forces and descend on the old woman. She refuses to apologise. N'Deye, the intellectual joins forces with these colonial agents and asks her to do as the chief of police asks her to do. It is now that Ramatoulaye realises that her granddaughter had obviously been trained to be a good interpreter of colonial values and outlook to her people. The narrating voice tells us that this time she does not allow N'Deye to even finish her sentence, that with the back of her hand, and without even turning to look at her, Ramatoulaye slaps her across the face, resulting in the girl falling backward from the bench and a thread of blood running from the corner of her mouth.

The physical act of violence becomes the symbol of Ramatoulaye's final but conscious rejection of the authority of those petty bourgeois elements, the likes of her own granddaughter, who had become captives of the colonial education system. With that Ramatoulaye can now give form and words to her thoughts. She can now speak for herself, interpret the world for herself, and be able to conceptualise in words, the class character of the colonial system. She speaks out for herself and says she would never apologise for opposing and acting against colonial thought and practice.

Imbued with this kind of consciousness, the women are now ideologically ready to march to Dakar, the very seat of colonial authority. They are ready to confront the colonial state. The woman who becomes the mind and heart of the great march to Dakar is Penda, another who has been transformed by her involvement in the social struggle. Penda moves from the individualism of a blanket anti-maleness to an affirmation of the creative value of the collective action of the oppressed. Initially, to her at least, men are all dogs. But gradually being drawn into the strike, she begins to see connections between gender oppression in a traditional patriarchy and the other issues of class and race domination under colonial capitalism. Once again it is the challenges arising from involvement in actions to change reality that end up changing the actors, in this case, Penda herself. The greatest growth for her comes in the conception, the execution of the march to Dakar. She is at the centre of it, the heart and the head of the march. But in another sense all the women are in it. The key thing is that the march is thought out and carried out by women. They have taken their initiative in a historical moment. Men help but the decisions are the women's, a far cry from the beginning of the strike and the narrative.

Nothing of course is achieved without sacrifice. Maïmouna the blind woman loses a child. Old Niakoro dies. Penda too. But the struggle changes their attitudes towards themselves, one another, their men, and the colonial system, but above all, to their self-conception as human beings. This is best symbolised by the death of Niakoro. From the position that the strike is simply the affair of men, she ends up in the midst of the fight against the colonial police. Struggles in the universities of organised struggle are the highest form of education, which leads to a critical consciousness that in turn leads to affirmative actions for change.

In a sense everybody who becomes involved in the strike is changed by that very attempt to change the colonial condition. Even at the individual level, there is a change of attitudes even among those who had previously thought of themselves as being progressive. Bakayoko ends up wanting to review his relationship with Assitan. Samba acknowledges that he is the father of Maïmouna's children. N'Deye burns all the racist literature she has been reading. Her real education has to start all over again.

The journey to collective awareness is not a smooth movement from one stage to the next in linear progression. The struggle as a whole brings out contradictions, which have to be faced by the characters before they can know themselves. There are contradictions between colonised blacks and colonial whites. But there are also contradictions between the real owners of capital in Paris and the colonial whites who are really just well-paid functionaries of the real bosses in Paris. Again among the whites, there are those who side with and even identify with the interests of the striking workers. Some of them even contribute money to the strike. Among the blacks, there are contradictions between men and women, between the various communities. Some of these can be overcome, because, in a sense, they are not antagonistic. But there are also clearly antagonistic relations that can never be overcome except through the defeat of one group by another: those between black workers as a whole, and the black bourgeois collaborators. The leaders of institutional religions, the assimilated deputies in French Parliament, and those like Beaugosse whose minds have been hopelessly messed up by the colonial racist culture. Contradictions are inherent in natural and social phenomena. And freedom is precisely the recognition of this necessity. Critical consciousness, transformation of the community, new relations emerge in the recognition of these contradictions and the struggle to overcome them through a consolidation of those which are not antagonistic to those conditions, classes, ideologies, and values that are clearly antagonistic to the real needs of the community.

The key thing is the consciousness that people can change the conditions of their being. And this is the main difference between Sembene Ousmane's novel and Zola's *Germinal*. The parallels in plot, character and incidents are too many and too similar for anybody not to see that Sembene had read *Germinal* and mastered it fully. But it is not plagiarism. The incidents and characters in *God's Bits of Wood* are too clearly embedded in

French colonised West Africa. The pages ooze with the reality of African life. It is interesting that the narrative itself is punctuated and to a certain extent framed by reference to orature.

Maïmouna, the blind woman, keeps on singing the legend of Goumba N'daiye. Goumba N'Daiye is the stubborn, beautiful woman of so many African stories. She will not marry just anybody. Whenever proposed to she challenges the suitor to a contest in working the fields. Many men flee from her demands of hard work in the fields. Then comes a stranger. And this time she meets somebody who, like her, does not easily give up. The man cannot quite vanquish the woman; neither can the woman; so eventually, they decide to combine their strengths against their enemies just as indeed, albeit through competition, they have already done against nature. And it is the last verse of the struggle in the ballad that actually ends Sembene's narrative. Thus the optimism in the oral ballad becomes also the optimism of the narrative of the anti-colonial struggle. The African past can be a source of strength in the struggles of the present for the future. The entire thrust of the narrative and the double endings of the ballad and the narrative shows that in the African worldview, people can change things, and this is a far cry from the naturalism and biological determinism of Emile Zola. People's actions are primary in the making of history! Sembene Ousmane's dialectics are a negation of Zola's biological determinism. Zola's biological determinism embodies despair; Sembene Ousmane's dialectical outlook and method embody hope.

The children in Sembene's work are a good example of this. From being merely a nuisance, they become active participants, their actions changing the course of the strike. Their alliance with Penda – the alliance of youth and women, the groups previously thought to have nothing to contribute to the affairs of the adult male population – has obvious revolutionary implications for the future. The novel, clearly and unequivocally, acknowledges and extols the role of the children in social struggles. In Sembene Ousmane's work, even in his films, there is always an image of a child, representing the future. If there is any way in which Ousmane differs from many African writers it is in his tremendous optimism best exemplified in *God's Bits of Wood* and embodied in the song of the blind woman about the legendary contest between Woman and Man but who, in the end, working together, are finally able to defeat their enemies.

The totality of his work, in print and visual media, is one of the greatest epical tributes to the capacity of the oppressed to change the conditions of their being and in the process change themselves. His work speaks of the possibilities of human freedom and is worth visiting and revisiting, for in every revisit the work yields more.

Voices & Icons
The Neocolonial
in Emergent African Cinema

Africa has been part of world cinema since its invention by the Lumière brothers in 1895. The early protodocumentaries of the Lumières and Méliès were shown in Algeria, Senegal and Egypt at about the same time that they were showing in Europe. The development of the cinema in Africa was shaped or more precisely misshapen by the historical moment in which the art was born. The invention of this great agent for the illusion of immortality came only ten years after the infamous Berlin conference which had divided Africa into spheres of influence and control of the various European powers. Thus the cinema came to Africa under colonial conditions. Colonialism laid the foundations. Cinema everywhere is part of an entire industry of the production, distribution and consumption of images. Right from the beginning Africa had absolutely no control or any say over the means of production of cinematic images either of its own territories or of other countries. The necessary technology, finance and distributive machinery remained with the racial descendants of the Lumières, the Méliès and the Edisons. Africa remained a consumer of images of itself and of other countries, but all of these images were produced, financed, and distributed from the various centres of Western empires.

For the empires, the cinematic icon came at a time when colonialists' literary and journalistic voices were already painting Africa in the darkest of colours. The racist image in the works of popular writers like Rider Haggard, and even in the more serious writers like Joseph Conrad, drew on similar images from the narratives of colonial explorers, looters, missionaries. The likes of Henry Morton Stanley, combining the roles of journalist, Christian emissary and trader had set the foundation and the tone of a tradition with such sensational titles as *In Darkest Africa*. It can be seen that even in the titles chosen there was the pictorial play with light and shadows. The illustrations in such texts are very telling: the white adventurer is always at the centre: light spreads from him to the outer darkness. The African crowds usually merged with the shadows.The framing of the characters to favour the white man as the centre of the action preceded the cinema. With its greater surface realism, however, the cinematic image could outdo the literary and journalistic voices in the depiction of the barbarity, the savagery, the infantilism, the docility, all the dark otherness that made white civilisation more luminous. Whiteness became more visibly splendid when juxtaposed against Blackness. The cinematic icon could conclusively give visual credence to the racist products of the voice, oral or literary, that preceded it. Thus Hegelian Africa, as a land of ravenous beasts and dangerous snakes still enveloped in the dark mantle of mere nature and inhabited by a people who had no connection with humanity, could be put on the screen. For the Hollywood tradition, Africa has always provided markets and esoteric backdrops. Tarzan's Africa and its variations remained the dominant image of Africa in Western features and documentaries whether sympathetic or not. So Africa remained a consumer of cinematic images.

The anti-colonial resistance gave rise to a great literature albeit largely in European languages. And right from the beginning it was a literature which was determined to correct the images of Africa in European literature. It varied in literary competence and in its understanding of the social forces at work. Some of the images of Africa it drew were not that different from those of the white missionaries or those in the books studied in the colonial classroom. But some other African writers, with Sembene and Alex la Guma leading the crowd, were to comprehend the march of history and to lay bare and naked colonialism in all its economic, political and cultural manifestations. The images of Africa that such literary voices drew were not those of a static Africa but of a continent being formed and reformed by struggle and resistance. This literature taken as a whole has created a debate within its ranks; it has confronted, head on, the issues deeply affecting colonial and postcolonial Africa. It is the nearest thing to a common pan-African property because many from all corners of the continent and from all walks of life can see themselves in it. The literary voices could accomplish this because the writers were in a more independent position vis-à-vis the means of literary production: one could always get pen and paper and write. Getting published and distributed was another matter. But even there, if the worst came to the worst, one could always circulate the images in their manuscript form. It is important to note that in this case the most liberated images in terms of production came from the voice in the tradition of orature. In orature one only needed the human voice box as the means of sounding out images. The means of production, distribution and consumption of images in the sung poem or narrative were always within the control of those opting for resistance. It is interesting that there are many instances where the colonial and even postcolonial authorities have tried to limit those sung images by banning the songs and the stories or imprisoning the bards. But even in prisons people carried within themselves the technologies for the production and distribution of images drawn by the voice.

Cinema was different. The means of production were not a matter of pen and paper or manuscripts that could be passed from hand to hand. Nor were they a matter of the human body being its own producer and instant distributor of images. Cinematic images involve very expensive technology, big money and political power. In the colonial era, there was no African cinema as an African-controlled industry or art form. There was only European cinema in Africa. And while the European and Hollywood cinema was part of Western hegemonic control, particularly in the area of cultural domination, African cinema was never an active part of the anti-colonial resistance for the simple reason that there was no African cinema at all.

African cinema, by which I mean cinema written, directed and acted by Africans, is strictly speaking a postcolonial phenomenon. The first African directed film, *Afrique sur Seine,* a twenty-minute long drama by Paulin Soumanou Vieyra, came out in 1955. As an industry controlled from within Africa it still does not yet exist in any meaningful sense except in Egypt. But as an art form, there are now enough films made by Africans for us to tentatively talk about the African cinema. However it still does not constitute a tradition with its own history of internal debate and commentary and schools, the kind of discourse we find in African orature and literature. If the absence of an African cinema in the past was a direct consequence of the colonial situation, its emergence in the postcolonial era is being affected by the historical space of its being and becoming.

The space is circumscribed by the neocolonial conditions of postcolonial Africa. Neocolonialism is a situation in which a country is formally politically independent in the sense of having a state whose legitimacy in international relations is not bound by the laws of another country, but whose economy, nevertheless, is controlled by the bourgeoisie of another state, in most cases, but not necessarily so, that of the former colonising power. The regimes of a neocolonial state see their role as that of guarding the economic interests of the West. Independence does not mean a fundamental change in the structures of the inherited colonial economy. Such regimes often end up being alienated from the general population, and in response they suppress the civil society often using the same methods as those used by the ex-colonial power. Their role is to ensure stability for the free operation of foreign capital, finance capital mostly. The fear of capital flight is like the legendary sword of Damocles. For these regimes democracy and any elements of self-organisation are anathema. They increasingly disregard any concerns raised from within the nation and they come to rely more on the bullet rather than the ballot. And because these regimes often get their financial, military and even political support from outside the nation, from the West mainly, they tend to be contemptuous of national initiatives and to look to the West for inspiration and approval. For their spiritual nourishment, the national social stratum that gains most from this neocolonial arrangement tends to look approvingly at the West or at the unthreatening remnants of precolonial cultures. Postcolonial Africa is full of military and authoritarian regimes of one kind or other; they are neither fully accountable to their nation nor to the legislatures of the West. Underdevelopment is rife in Africa; and most neocolonial regimes in Africa are characterised by the presence of many donor agencies and certain areas of development are defined by these donor agencies.

Cinema is affected by this lopsided development. Quite often the regimes do not see any urgency in the matter for they are quite happy to buy and enjoy the images manufactured abroad including images of their own countries provided they have the legitimacy of having been produced in Hollywood. The cinema encouraged is that of a glossy Europe and America; or that of an Africa seen through Western eyes. And the images of Africa through Western eyes are themselves no more than a repackaging of images of colonial narratives. The postcolonial era has seen

Hollywood literally dredge through the racist narratives of the colonial era and come up with films like *King Solomon's Mines* based on the work of Rider Haggard, or *Mister Johnson* based on the novels of Joyce Cary, or *The Flame Trees of Thika* based on the work of the Kenya white settler spokeswoman, Elspeth Huxley. Is there a kind of nostalgia for the colonial era? Yes, because a story like *King Solomon's Mines* has been made and re-made three times in 1937, 1950 and in 1984. Perhaps the best known of this trend in the eighties and nineties is Sydney Pollock's Film, *Out of Africa*.

This film was based on the book of the same title by the Danish colonial settler in Kenya, Karen Blixen alias Isaak Dinesen. Karen Blixen lived in Kenya between 1914 and 1933. Her account of those years is full of the crudest racist descriptions of African peoples but ironically in a very elegant prose full of protestations about her love for the continent, its fauna and flora, its wild animals and of course its Africans. For Karen Blixen, these Africans who in childhood are more precocious than European children of the same age, suddenly and mysteriously come to a standstill in their mental development at the ages of 13 for the darkest skins and 17 for the lightest. So according to the testimony in her book, *Shadows on the Grass,* these adult Africans who worked for her had the mentalities of European children at the ages of 13 and 17. And as she loved boys and wild animals, it was not difficult for her to love these children whatever their ages were! In fact, so she says, what she had learnt from the wild animals of Africa was actually very useful to her in dealing with the Africans. The film avoided the more racist statements from the book. And the photographic realism captures the surface beauty of the Kenyan landscape. But in its very realism, it endorses a more basic lie. A group of Kenyans who saw the film in Sweden wrote in protest:

Nowhere in the film are Kenyans depicted as showing any resistance to colonialism. On the contrary they are shown as being quite happy with the colonial set up. They sing happily as they work for Karen Blixen on the very land taken away from them by the colonial state and given to Blixen for a pittance. A colonial appointed chief, actually a traitor to his people, a Chief Kenyanjui, is depicted as an authentic African chief. Was there not even a single African who was unhappy about working on the land that had been taken from his own people?

The film, like so many other revivals, glosses over the brutality of colonialism and also over the facts of African people's resistance to sell a more acceptable face of colonialism. This is quite consonant with the neocolonial mood. Colonialism was not that bad after all. Glossy Europe and glamourised West; geographic magazine Africa; colonial themes dressed up a little and imported back into Africa as contemporary cinema.

But how has the emergent African cinema been dealing with this historical moment? There are two broad patterns that one can discern. There is the trend represented by Sembene Ousmane and Haile Gerima. This takes the neocolonial conditions seriously and examines the African being under conditions of struggle and resistance. Their Africa, distorted by years of imperialist loot and plunder from the days of slavery to the present, has managed to survive and to overcome the many odds against it. This is the spirit of Africa that they celebrate. Sembene Ousmane's stand for instance is uncompromisingly that of the working majority. From *The Black Girl* to *Gelwaar* he has been very consistent in examining the contradictions between Africa as a whole and the West; and also within African societies. In the case of Haile Gerima every frame is full of the tension of struggle. *Sankofa,* his film on slavery is worth more than all the history books which have been written on the subject. Out of that brutality, out of that unspeakable inhumanity, emerges an unbowed Africa, splendid in its defiant beauty. In this tradition are others like Med Hondo. His film *Sarraounia* celebrates African resistance with women at the centre. Every single film by these giants of the African cinema is worth viewing and studying over and over again. They are defining an African aesthetic of resistance and remarkable courage. And yet within Africa one is not likely to find their films in the major commercial houses or on the television screens at prime or other times.

The other trend is one of accommodation and compromise. Sometimes this trend is not even aware of its own politics. By this I mean that the viewer can see the good intentions; the writer-directors are sincere, but quite often they don't seem to be aware of the political implications of the image. The excitement of being behind the camera; of vividly capturing movement and voices and landscape on the frame; of the expectation of the big screen – these seem to be overwhelming. Nothing illustrates the two trends better than *The Heritage* directed by the Ghanaian director, Kwaw Ansah, and *Saikati* by the first major director from Kenya, Anne Mungai.

Ansah's first major release, *Love Brewed in an African Pot,* had made headlines wherever in Africa it was shown. In Nairobi Kenya there were queues and queues of Africans waiting patiently to buy their tickets. Some saw it several times. That was in the seventies. And then in the eighties he made another film, *The Heritage,* and released it to high acclaim. The film examines the anti-colonial resistance but it is quite clear that he is using themes located in colonialism and anti-colonial struggles to talk about the postcolonial Africa. One of the most poignant moments is when a member of the rising African petty bourgeoisie is given a precious piece of sculpture by his mother. The piece carries the heritage of his people. He is therefore charged to keep it, guard it, take care of it so that he too might in future pass it on to his children to keep and continue the family history and secrets. Our good African, very highly educated, takes the sculpture to the White Governor who is fond of collecting African art.

The governor examines the piece, admires it, and to the horror of any viewer who understands the implications, the African gentleman tells him: 'It's for you. You can keep it, sir!' Even the Governor is a little surprised by this act of senseless generosity. How could a person give away the heritage of his own people to a stranger? This is the class which later, at Independence, takes on the heritage of struggle, the beautiful gift of Independence, and then turns it into a neocolonial affair. However, the aesthetic of the film is clearly in the tradition of struggle and resistance and affirmation of what is enduring and true in the story of African survival.

Saikati was released in 1993. It was directed by a young Kenyan woman, Anne Mungai, and it is the first feature to be made in Kenya, directed by a Kenyan, acted by Kenyans with a largely Kenyan crew. So the very act of producing it is a historic breakthrough particularly in Kenya where the landscape has been used so often by Hollywood. *Saikati* tells the story of a young schoolgirl who runs away from a Maasai home because her parents want her to marry the son of a chief. This would mean that quite apart from being given to a man she does not love, a marriage would see the end of her schooling. But she enjoys school and she has hopes of one day becoming a doctor. She runs away to Nairobi with a cousin with promises of a job and therefore a chance of continuing with her education. In the city we see her transformation from a rural Maasai girl into a modern city woman. But the work she is expected to do is one of sleeping with white tourists. Saikati refuses and she struggles to keep her dignity despite the negative example of her cousin who, after being jilted by her African boyfriend, has no qualms prostituting herself for survival. Eventually Saikati decides to go back to her rural home. Nairobi does not quite deliver on the promises. Two white tourists agree to take her back to her Maasai home – how generous of them! On the way back the foursome – the two cousins and the two white men – drive through a Kenya landscape of luxurious hotels and dramatic game reserves. At one time Saikati and her erstwhile would-be seducer get lost in the Kenyan jungle of wonderful fauna and flora, really Karen Blixen's landscape, and they have to find their way to the Maasai place without of course the help of their more knowledgeable friends. They are now all alone, thrown together by circumstances. Strong feelings are developing between the tourist and the Maasai girl, or is it love? Eventually they reach the neighbourhood of her Maasai home. Saikati goes into a little bush and changes into her Maasai costumes, colourful beads and all that. She is once again transformed from a city woman into a rural Maasai woman. Then comes a poignant moment in the narrative almost reminiscent of the Ansah's *The Heritage*. But the similarities end there. Saikati takes out a very special necklace made of beautiful of beads. Colours and beadwork are central to Maasai aesthetics and communication. It is often by the arrangement of colours that one can tell the clan to which the wearer belongs. 'This contains all the dreams of our people,' she tells her white companion. Please take it. There is definite approval for this act in the film. The shots are arranged to suggest intimacy and gratitude. The two have made a human contact that transcends race and tourism. Love transcends colour even if this means giving the symbol of all the dreams of one's people to a stranger. Thus whereas in Kwaw Ansah's film there is disapproval, a criticism of the sale of national heritage by the postcolonial state, in Mungai's case there is approval, a clear visual endorsement of the act.

Other films fall between the two trends. The very able film, *Neria,* by a new Zimbabwean director, Godwin Mawuru, released in 1993, has a white 'Rhodesian' judge arbitrating between an

African family. Law here emerges as a neutral force above race, class and gender. What the women need do is to know their rights and then have the courage to file lawsuits against those who would use traditionalism as a tool of oppression. This is not to say that white judges cannot arbitrate in the domestic affairs of an African family. This is the reality of Zimbabwe as indeed it is of many former white settler colonies like Kenya, as the majority of the occupants of the judicial benches are white. But the problem with the film is that it makes no attempt to situate this within the historical realities of a Zimbabwe where until very recently apartheid type racism was the norm. Have all the racial tensions gone with the wind of Independence? A shot or two, a rearrangement of some *mis-en-scène* could so easily have rectified the bias and corrected the view of Zimbabwe as a land of racial harmony except for patriarchal traditionalism. Thus the film, so admirable in the way it focuses on the abuses of patriarchy and the need for women to assert themselves and demand their rights, becomes flawed when situated in the totality of Zimbabwean politics. Without so intending, the director gives us a picture of Zimbabwe that is not consonant with its recent history where Independence was won through the barrel of the gun wielded by Zimbabwean guerrillas.

In the Burundian film, *Gito, l'ingrat* (Gito the Ungrateful), directed by Léonce Ngabo, a white girl who is being deceived by her African boyfriend flies to Africa to see what he is up to. She finds out that he is engaged in other liaisons. From the moment she lands in Burundi, all the crucial initiatives are with her. She teams up with the family of the boyfriend and also with his African girlfriend. The two girls decide to avenge themselves against the culprit. Once again, she is the leader, with the African woman merely a follower. Eventually she flies back to Belgium after successfully devising and carrying out a scheme for publicly humiliating the boyfriend. She came, she saw, she conquered, and then she left. Towards the end, the boyfriend is transformed; he is chastened and will no doubt keep his appetite for women under control; and more importantly, he no longer aspires to join the civil service bureaucracy. In the film the problems of postcolonial Africa are reduced to the facts of the educated refusing to take up humbler skills leading to ultimately more useful jobs, like sewing or carpentry. The task of running the administration and big business can be left in the hands of the Belgians. Booker T. Washington of *Up From Slavery* is not dead after all. He is being resurrected in African film. Not that this is what the director is consciously trying to say. He has a point about the colonial education conditioning the educated into despising manual labour and looking down upon the peasantry who actually do the real production. And we do see this in the film. Gito the ungrateful does not even want to go to his village. On arrival from Europe, he checks into a modern hotel in the city. But when the girl from Belgium comes onto the scene she emerges as a Miss-know-it-all. She has no problem in going to the countryside and working as a peasant on the land. In Belgium, we never see her working on the land of course and we never see her in a factory using her hands. In Africa the film does not present an African woman who could have offered an alternative to the lifestyle for which Gito initially opts.

The danger for young African film makers who do not come from a tradition of resistance may well lie in their being seduced into thinking that the entertainment value is everything; that National Geographic type of images are everything; that to succeed, they must abandon social themes and reach out for an abstract internationalism. African cinema would gain much if the film makers were to connect themselves to the progressive aspects of African literature. Some of the battles being fought out in African cinema were settled in African literature long ago; and it is frankly quite disconcerting to see African films being made as if Oyono, Beti and Sembene had never written any novels about colonialism or as if there had never been any debates about negritude.

In the area of African languages, however, African cinema and the vibrant Nollywood film and video industry have taken the lead over African literature. It is vitally important for Africans to see themselves on the screen and to hear their own voices. The Hollywood screen has degraded African languages. When some characters are made to utter African words, it often does not matter to the Hollywood screen what the words mean as long as the noises being made sound like something which is not recognisably European. Even alien creatures from outer space are sometimes given a few words from African languages. So by making African characters speak in African languages with English or French subtitles, African cinema is subverting the tradition of Europhone African literature and theatre which creates characters who speak perfect English and French.

It also undermines the negative representations of African languages on the Hollywood screen.

This is important because the cinema has the greatest illusion of realism. In some ways the cinematic icon is more powerful than the literary voice in its immediacy and its directness. Questions of representation and of the democratic accessibility to the means of producing those representations should be a matter of involved debate. Even questions of form should be a matter of concern and debate. By its very immediacy and photographic realism, stories that people would not ordinarily regard as particularly interesting or intellectually stimulating, are rendered more acceptable on the screen. A lie in the cinema can be more damaging than all the other lies in the other icons and voices for it is a lie often dressed up as realism.

The emergent African cinema is struggling against great odds. It has often had to depend on donor agencies; on the ministries of cooperation of the West; and on festivals as venues. Many African states are indifferent to its emergence; after all the screens as they are now carry their favourite items made in the West. African cinema has no slot in the national television networks. The cinema houses also tend to be owned by multinationals.

I am however convinced that, even within these limitations, its greatest strength will come from its conscious alliance with struggles for survival and from its being faithful to its primary audiences in Africa. It will become alive if and when it becomes total cinema, representing all the contradictions of Africa from the economic and the political to the cultural and the most spiritual, personal and intimate. That day is coming! And this transformation has been facilitated by the digital revolution: for these technologies are democratising access to the means of production of visual images, of moving images. First video cameras, then digital cameras with their more immediate production methods and desk-top editing, removed the mystique and expense of film editing. And as the success of the Nollywood industry in Nigeria – and its parallel industries in other parts of Africa have demonstrated, the technology itself can move African cinema to a new place – as the video/DVD image does not even require a public space for screening – one's own home will do!

Birth of a Nation
Narrating the National Question
in Pepetela's* *Mayombe*

Pepetela *Mayombe*
(Translated from the Portuguese by Michael Wolfers; London:
Heinemann AWS 269 1983; Harare: Zimbabwe Publishing
House ZPH Writers Series 1983)
—— *Mayombe* (Lisboa: Edições 70 1980)

Modern Angolan Literature was born in the field of political
struggle and particularly in the armed phase. More actively than
their counterparts in English- and- French-speaking Africa, the
elite in Angola were very involved in the militant struggle against
colonialism. Many were active members of MPLA. They were
to be found in the various levels of the party organisation, in
the diplomatic missions, in prisons, and in the urban and rural
guerrilla armies. Pepetela, one of the better known novelists
from Angola, sets his narrative *Mayombe* almost entirely in the
guerrilla camps, with a wealth of details that could only have
come from a person with first-hand experience.[1] Written in 1971
it was published after independence. This was appropriate: many
of the issues that confront the characters in *Mayombe* bear on
the fate and destiny of the struggle and of the country; and they
anticipate with unerring clarity the problems of the postcolonial
era. The forces of nationalism, democracy and socialism, the

---

* Pepetela, pen-name of Artur Carlos Mauricio Pestana.
[1] In the translator's preface to the 1983 Heinemann edition of the novel, Michael Wolfers
says that the author served in Cabinda.

organisation of power at the party and state levels, are pertinent issues for Angola and the world. These forces have changed the face of the twentieth century; and the questions of power in a one-party socialist state anticipate the current international debate occasioned by the collapse of Eastern European states in the 1980s. These issues evolve out of the main concern in the narrative: the forging of a national consciousness among the various communities that make up Angola, a process involving many contradictions.

The first and the most obvious is that of the nation and its ethnic components. But are they components or opponents? One of the more obvious effects of Imperialism was to bring into the same economic, political and administrative orbit various communities, often with different languages and different historical experiences. It also divided others into the spheres of control of different colonial powers. In short many African communities were herded together into one territory; yoked under one economic system, tongue-tied under one official common language of the colonial power within a newly named space. Did this mean the colonial invention of new nations? Some African intellectuals have bought into the coloniser's view of themselves and have written as if colonialism created new nations out of undesirable warring ethnic components. They see this as one of the benefits of colonialism. But did Imperialist colonialism really create new nations in Africa?

The new postcolonial nations were not formed by colonialism. On the contrary, new nations develop out of their struggle against external control, against the colonial state, against colonialism. This is one of the major differences between the rise of new nations in Africa and Europe. European nations, post-renaissance nations, rose in their struggle against feudalism and the religious hegemony of the Catholic church. But they also emerged from their struggles against one another. Modern

European nations were created by capitalist and colonialist rivalries. Thus while colonialism helped the invention of new nations in Europe and America, in Africa colonialism clearly tried to prevent the emergence and growth of new nations. Frantz Fanon has made the apt observation that colonialism, for the colonised was, by its very structure, separatist and regionalist.[2] The colonial state actively encouraged rivalries between the various communities; they invented the phenomenon known as tribalism and prevented any associations that encompassed the territory as a whole and in the case of political parties would only allow regionally based political formations, if any. In most countries in Africa political parties formed on the basis of the entire territory were allowed only a year or so before the handing over of power. The nature of colonial economies is one of uneven development. The more developed regions were played off against underdeveloped ones with the colonial state often acting as arbiter. Workers drawn into the capital from all parts of the country were often denied residential rights. They were permanent immigrants, contract workers, legally and formally still tied to their region and community of origin. In a thousand and one ways, colonialism did everything possible to prevent the emergence of a consciousness of common origins and a common destiny among the colonised, preferring, on the contrary, to deal with each region separately and to play one against the other. Yoked together and yet being made to see themselves as separate units, that is the story of colonial peoples. In such a situation, the forging of a national consciousness is one wrought with many problems. The most important problem is still that of ethnic identities which, emptied of their precolonial content, became actively fostered by colonialism as forms of regional

---

[2] Frantz Fanon *The Wretched of the Earth* (New York 1991, p. 94. First published in French in 1961 as *Les Damnés de la Terre,* Preface by Jean-Paul Sartre. Translated by Constance Easington; New York: Grove Press 1963).

nostalgia. How does a national movement overcome the rivalries, the suspicions, of those ethnic communities?

Mayombe is a microcosm of the whole of Angola and Africa. The characters, all are under the umbrella of MPLA and come from the different ethnicities which make up Angola. They are opening a new front in Cabinda. They face a common enemy and a common danger in the forest. But at the beginnings of the operations in *Mayombe*, they are depicted as living in separate ethnic camps. The complexity of the ethnic and racial scene in Angola from which a national consciousness has to emerge is boldly depicted in a description of the men in the camp who often interact only within the social boundaries defined by their ethnicity. They fall into two large ethnic groups: the Kimbundus in one 'camp' and all the others, the Kikongos, the Umbundus, and those that do not fit into any specific ethnic label in another. For example, Muatianvua, born in Luanda of an Umbundu father and a Kimbundu mother. The Operations Chief, third in command, for instance, dwells in a reality coloured by ethnicity. It is in his thoughts and actions and those of Miracle that the limiting effects of ethnic consciousness are dramatised. The thoughts of Miracle, the Bazooka man, a Kimbundu, are initially depicted as being completely on the level of ethnic consciousness. For him the Cabindas are dangerous by the very virtue of their being Cabindans. His father, a poor peasant, was killed by the Portuguese and he tends to see loyalties to the movement and people's characters in terms of their degree of victimisation: for him, the Kimbundus have suffered more under the whites and therefore they should be, by virtue of their ethnic origins, the ones calling the shots. Political arguments between the Military Commander and the Political Commissar, are seen by those less politically clear through the eyes of their ethnic consciousness.

Pepetela's text also raises the problem that most bedevils the emergence of a national consciousness, the language factor. But the text prevaricates over this question, at least over the solution. When the guerrilla unit captures some workers employed by the Portuguese, and Struggle offers to speak to the captives in Fiote, this offer is refused in favour of Portuguese. What is not fully explored or discussed in the text are the factors that have brought the people to this position where they distrust what is spoken in African languages and take shelter or show more faith in the languages of their tormentors. It is the political and cultural policies of the colonial state, the same policies that have nurtured 'tribalism' which have ensured the emergence of Portuguese, or a variation of it, as the only language spoken across the various communities. It is the official language. It is the language of power and education. African languages are not developed. They are not encouraged in the classroom. Any communication made between African languages is in fact so *despite* rather than *because of* the actions of the colonial state. Is it surprising that Portuguese becomes the only arbitrating presence when Angolans of the different communities are gathered together? It is also a fact that the leadership of many anti-colonial movements comes from the middle-class, educated in the language of the coloniser; and Angola is no different. The literate understand each other across their ethnic and racial origins, and they may often confuse their capacity to talk to each other as constituting the ability of all Angolans to speak to one another. They may even come to take it that Portuguese and other foreign languages are capable of replacing African languages as the vehicles of the national consciousness. They take the historical, mainly colonial, emergence of European languages into positions of power as inevitable.

It is an illusion shared by even the most progressive of African intellectuals. Some prominent African writers for instance have expressed their gratitude to colonialism for the gift of the English language. In December 1995, and despite the raging debate about African languages, the Congolese writer and Deputy-Director of

Unesco public relations and former Prime Minister of Congo-Brazzaville, Henri Lopès, could still write, in an article carried in *Jeune Afrique*, that French was no longer a foreign language in Africa, that it was, in fact, now, an African language, by implication, even more African than African languages since it could do things for Africa that African languages could never do: bring about a national or supranational consciousness. Stating that for him Francophonie constituted one language, one family, and one politics, he goes on to say: 'Even if it is not a language of African origin, French is no longer a foreign language in the continent: it is henceforth an African language.'[3]

The fact is Congo has its African languages. French is a foreign language, a colonial language, although it is the language of the Congolese elite, the ruling establishment, taken as a whole. But it is not the Congolese elite and the ruling establishment who constitute the Congolese nation! It is the millions of others, with their different African languages. The self image of the African educated and the ruling establishment can only be found in the mirror of European languages. In the mirror of their own African languages, they see only the darkness of tribal marks and rivalries; and darkness does not reflect light! But for millions of the majority their African languages were able to mirror correctly the nature of colonialism and the need for unity to fight it: hence some of the most successful political parties were the ones that espoused unity and consistent anti-imperialism.

In the same way four hundred years of Portuguese domination has not made Portuguese the common language of everyday speech, the language of popular culture. African languages still exist and remain, despite the blows, the actual languages of

---

[3] '*La francophonie c'est pour moi tout à la fois une langue, une famille et, peut-être, une politique.*' '*Même si elle n'est pas une langue d'origine Africaine, le français n'est plus une langue étrangère dans le continent, c'est desormais une langue Africaine.*' Henri Lopès 'Francophonie: demain, peut-etre...', *Jeune Afrique* No 1822, 7 to 13 December 1995, p. 25.

culture. Nevertheless, it is easier to foster mutual suspicions when a people do not speak a common language.

This is brought out very well in the text. The suspicions are real, but they are, like all the other divide-and-rule tactics, rooted in a history whose negation is precisely the one being worked out in the national liberation struggle. A common language would of course largely facilitate communications and allay some of the unfounded fears. The text recognises the need for a common language as a uniting factor. Portuguese is seen as constituting that language because it is more or less understood across the elites of the various national communities. Yet the problem remains and the national movement will have to come up with a policy that recognises that African peoples have languages and those languages, like the communities and regions and cultures that created them are part of the overall national heritage.[4]

An aspect of ethnicity confronted by the text is the issue of products of inter-racial love. It is through the character and thoughts of Theory, 'the one in-between' as he calls himself, that this aspect is most dramatised. Theory's father was a Portuguese trader and his mother a black woman. Theory is haunted by the fear of rejection. He wants to belong but on what basis of belonging? 'When I was still a child, I wanted to be white, so that whites would not call me black. As a man, I wanted to be black so that blacks would not hate me,'[5] he confesses, at least to himself. He is ruled by the need to prove that he can be trusted. Therefore he is ruled by fear and by implication he is, at the beginning, also living on the level of ethnic consciousness. The racial and ethnic complexes are what all the people will have to overcome before the national consciousness can take root. Theory is in

---

[4] For further discussions on the language issue in Africa, see my books *Decolonising the Mind* and *Moving the Centre* both published by James Currey Ltd, EAEP Ltd and Heinemann Inc. And for a plurality of voice on the same, see the special issue of *Research in African Literatures*, Fall 1991.

[5] Pepetela *Mayombe* (London: Heinemann AWS 269 1983, p. 5).

fact used, in the narrative, as a symbol of the transcendence over the extremities of opposites: 'In a Universe of yes or no, white or black, I represent the maybe.'[6] Is there room for a maybe in a world that seems to him too Manichean, too hopelessly locked in a struggle of neat opposites?

Overall, it is action, the revolutionary practice of anti-colonial struggle, that is seen as the positive mediating factor. Often this involves violence and therefore the readiness to die for Angola. It is not simply the claims of being Angolan that makes one an Angolan, but rather the readiness to redeem Angolans from colonial hell. The awakening to a national consciousness is dramatised in the snake incident where the guerrilla group, thinking that they are being attacked by the enemy forces, react with a sense of a common mission and purpose. Ethnicity seems to disappear in the face of a common danger and the concrete action necessary to counter it. This elicits nothing but praise from Fearless who observes that they had at that moment forgotten their various tribal origins, had forgotten inconveniences and the danger of the action, they had all become volunteers, ready to face whatever threatened them as Angolans:

> That's why I have confidence in the Angolans. They are muddlers, but they all forget their quarrels and spites to rescue a companion from danger. That is the merit of the Movement, to have achieved the miracle of beginning to transform men. Another generation and the Angolan will be a new man. What is needed is action.[7]

The action of the novel then shows two things: that a national consciousness has to evolve through concrete actions of struggle both against the Portuguese and the divisive inheritance of their colonial history. It is in the process of working together, waging a struggle against a common enemy, that a national consciousness

---

[6] Ibid., p. 1 (Heinemann 1996 edition).
[7] Ibid., p. 151.

is born. It takes a long time because there are centuries of colonial divisionary tactics and their effects to overcome. But revolutionary actions, the actions to overturn the conditions of exploitation, oppression and cultural subjugation are the real and final basis of a triumphant national consciousness. The narrative in fact ends with precisely that affirmation. When Struggle and the Military Commander die in action, an action aimed at relieving the hard-pressed Political Commissar, the lesson is brought home to all the participants and it is interesting that it is the Operations Chief who now articulates the lessons learnt:

> Struggle, who was Cabinda, died to save a Kimbundu. Fearless, who was Kikongo, died to save a Kimbundu. It is a great lesson for us, comrades.[8]

The main thesis developed in the novel is clear: the necessity of a national consciousness that transcends ethnic identities. But it is a process, not often easy to come by, a product of a long protracted struggle against a common enemy and also against the divisive tendencies of negative ethnic identities and consciousness among those fighting against the enemy. If the contradictions between the common enemy and the Angolan Communities as a whole are not resolved through democratic practices and dialogue – an impossibility in a colonial situation – then they will only be resolved through armed revolutionary violence. Equally, if the contradictions among the colonised are not resolved through dialogue and democratic practices, they will also lead to arms and violence, and in this case reactionary violence. And it is a fact of history that after Independence, civil war did break out between the social forces and tendencies represented by UNITA under Savimbi and those represented by MPLA, to the detriment of Angola's healthy national recovery and a further impediment to the maturing of that long process of national consciousness.

[8] Ibid., p. 183.

Thus at any one moment a political struggle for a national consciousness can generate into a revolutionary armed struggle against the common enemy or degenerate into reactionary ethnic warfare among those struggling. Both situations invite a consideration of the role of violence in the anti-colonial struggle.

The question of violence and its role in generating a positive national consciousness or degenerating into negative ethnic consciousness is central to the narrative. Is violence regenerative or destructive? The narrative seems to be an examination of the Fanonistic thesis about the role of violence in the decolonisation process advanced in his major work, *The Wretched of the Earth*. But it takes issues with some of the formulation of the problem, the solutions suggested and the results anticipated. The starting point is of course the violence of the colonial state.

Fanon sees the entire colonial system as being permeated by violence; its very being, theory and practice are those of violence. As he graphically puts it, the frontiers between the world of the settler and the native population in the colonial world are shown by the barracks and police stations.[9] Even if the native population were to try and forget about it, these agents of government who speak the language of pure force are omnipresent with their rifle-butts and napalm. They bring 'violence into the home and the mind of the native'.[10] Into the home, the violence is physical; and into the mind, it is psychological. Colonialism, he concludes, 'is violence in its natural state, and it will only yield when confronted with greater violence.'[11]

National liberation then becomes the process of meeting one kind of violence, an anti-people violence, with another, a pro-

---

[9] Frantz Fanon, op. cit., p. 38. 'The colonial world is a world cut in two. The dividing line, the frontiers are shown by barracks and police stations. In the colonies it is the policeman and the solder who are the official, the instituted go-between, the spokesmen of the settler and his rule of oppression.'

[10] Ibid.

[11] Ibid., p. 61

people violence.[12] He in fact comes very close to absolutising the effects of anti-imperialist violence when he says that the native finds his freedom only through violence. Violence is raised to a level where it is seen as the midwife of the nation bringing the various groups together. They recognise each other and the future nation is born.[13] Violence in action was all inclusive and national and it was closely involved in the liquidation of regionalism and of tribalism.[14] Its effects are even raised to an aesthetic and religious plane when he sees the aesthetic and cleansing effects of anti-imperialist violence:

> At the level of individuals violence is a cleansing force. It frees the native from his inferiority complex and from his despair and inaction; it makes him fearless and restores his self-respect.[15]

Whether a people embark on the stage of armed struggle is not a matter of choice. Often the colonial state presents them with no other choice. The armed struggle mobilises the people but it is because its very success depends on a politically mobilised people. It is the mobilisation that comes first. So the fanonistic doctrine still raises the fundamental question: is violence in and of itself a mobilising factor and a cleansing act? It is in this context that the discussion between the Military Commander, the Operations Chief and the Political Commissar,

[12] Ibid., pp. 35-7. Frantz Fanon's entire chapter 'Concerning Violence' is an illustration of that thesis.

[13] Ibid., p. 93. 'The appearance of the settler has meant in the terms of syncretism the death of the aboriginal society, cultural lethargy and the petrification of individuals. For the native, life can only spring up again out of the rotting corpse of the settler. This then is the correspondence, term by term, between the two trains of reasoning. But it so happens for the colonized people this violence, because it constitutes their only work, invests their characters with positive and creative qualities. The practice of violence binds them together as a whole, since each individual forms a violent link in the great chain, a part of the great organism of violence, which has surged upward in reaction to the settlers' violence in the beginning. The groups recognize each other and the future nation is born. The armed struggle mobilizes the people...'

[14] Ibid., p. 94.

[15] Ibid.

the three commanding officers of the Mayombe detachment, becomes important. The group of guerrillas under the command of the three officers have entered Mayombe in Cabinda and they have spotted a group of men working for a Portuguese timber company. The question arises as to what they should do about the situation. Should they raid them, capture and destroy their instruments and re-educate the captive workers? Or should they simply wait for a chance to engage the enemy soldiers and kill as many as possible? What arises particularly in the arguments between the Political Commissar and the Operations Chief is a clash between politics and militaristics.

As they are soldiers, argues the Operations Chief, the first action in the area has to be military. They should wait for the most optimum condition to ambush and kill significant numbers of enemy soldiers. But the Political Commissar argues that a people's war is not measured by the number of enemy dead but by the degree of popular support that it generates. The Operations Chief counters by arguing that this support is won through weapons alone. And then the Political Commissar comes up with a rejoinder that could be an answer to, or at least, a most important elaboration and modification of the Fanonistic doctrine:

> Not [with weapons] alone. With two things. With weapons and by politicization. We must first show that we are not bandits, that we do not kill the people. The people here don't know us, have heard only enemy propaganda, are afraid of us. If we take the workers, treat them well, discuss with them, and then later have a good go at the tuga, that way, certainly, the people will begin to believe and to accept us. But it is slow work.[16]

It is a question as to whether the gun follows politics or politics

---

[16] Pepetela *Mayombe*, pp. 12-13.

the gun, political education versus militarism.[17] In the phrase, 'armed struggle', the subject is 'struggle', and 'armed' is the qualification. It is arms in support of a just political struggle. The regeneration that Fanon talks about is that of organised armed struggle in support of the politics of total economic, political and cultural transformation of society so that those who were Last, the majority of the working population irrespective of race, religion and gender, could come First.

The enemy does not watch the forces of the anti-colonial struggle move into ascendancy without his trying to undermine their unity by appealing to and often allying with forces that have not gone beyond the stage of ethnic consciousness to embrace all the oppressed communities under the same territory. Colonialism survives though the active generation of internalised disputes among the oppressed, a phenomenon which, in Africa, often went under the misnomer of Black on Black Violence in the ghettoes, or on the territorial scale, civil war by a separatist region, often claiming to represent some regionally defined ethnic interests. Colonialism which had condemned certain regions and communities to virtual developmental neglect, then

---

[17] The fictional debate is here reminiscent of the debate of the foco theory of guerrilla warfare as advanced by Che Guevara and popularised in the Western media by Regis Debray. The idea was that in a colonial situation where the conditions were ripe for a revolution, a small group could take up arms, and become the centre or focal point of political awakening, organisation and general uprising. This was in contrast to the argument that political organisation and mobilisation were necessary conditions for armed guerrilla struggle.

A similar debate seems to have taken place in Zanu in Zimbabwe. In their book *The Struggle for Zimbabwe,* David Martin and Phyllis Johnson, have commented thus: 'In the sixties, there had been a tendency among some liberation movements, and particularly Zimbabwean movements, to believe that all that was necessary to end white minority domination was to train some guerrillas and send them home with guns: this would not only scare the whites but would ignite a wave of civil disobedience by blacks. Zanu explained the failure of the Sinoia battle for this inadequate attention to mobilisation of the people so that they could become the celebrated Maoist waters to the guerrilla fish. It was Tongorara trained in China in 1966 who brought home the lesson: "If you want to win a revolution it is not only the revolution of the gun but a revolution of mobilising the masses"' (p.11).

suddenly becomes the champion of these regions and peoples against real or imagined future discrimination by the forces that claim to represent a national consciousness.

And that is also why, on the whole, it is those forces from among the colonised who have been collaborating with the enemy who resort to the kind of violence that is also encouraged by the enemy. A great lesson yes, but one that was not learnt soon enough by all the forces, outside the fictional world of *Mayombe*. The war between MPLA and UNITA was to break out soon after MPLA took over power. It was not until 1995 – twenty years after formal independence – that a peace agreement was signed. But the civil war confirms more than it negates the general thesis in *Mayombe*. A prophetic merit of the novel was its virtual prediction of this UNITA v MPLA post-independence outcome in the arguments and attitudes of those participating in the Cabinda venture even though under the umbrella of MPLA. The novel is almost a warning against this kind of outcome for it was a recipe for effectively holding back the progressive and integrative development of a national consciousness. Violence in a colonial context can be divided into two: revolutionary violence that sets out to transform society and its internal relations; and conservative reactionary violence that sets up to maintain the status quo of inequalities or split up the emergent national movement.

The third set of contradictions emerging in the narrative is that of democracy, socialism and the one party state. Here it is clear that the narrative may have gained from what was happening in the rest of the continent which had already attained independence. The narrative addresses itself to the question of the organisation and operation of power in a postcolonial era. The debate between Commander Fearless and the Political Commissar is a frank discussion of these problems of the Party, Power and the People after armed victory. Fearless is warning against the possibility of the party in power turning against itself and the revolution. A party that gets strong on the basis of its connection with the people could easily turn into a church where only the elect are admitted and where the leadership could assume the position of the unerring clerics, and who, if they err and they do err, cannot criticise themselves or be criticised by others publicly. Whereas in the struggle, debate and discussion were encouraged at all the levels of the Party, after independence, and especially after it becomes apparent that the fruits of independence do not ripen overnight, the leadership may become impatient of any type of criticism. They will become sensitive to criticism and even excommunicate those who do not fit in the camp of 'yes, the leader and the party are always right':

> When you are in the seat of power, belonging to the narrow group that will control the Party and the State, after the first disillusionment of observing that socialism is not a task for one day and the will of a thousand men.[18]

Fearless warns against the dangers of a single party being seized by ambitious caterers of individual self-interest who may use the genuine and necessary need to tighten vigilance and discipline in the party to steel itself against counter-revolution as a cover, confusing counter-revolutionaries with all those who criticise personal ambitions and mistakes of the party and the leadership. In a party governed by the principles of Democratic Centralism, 'centralism is strengthened, democracy disappears'.[19] The narrative sees such an outcome as tragedy and here the criticism of a postcolonial state corresponds to that of Frantz Fanon in the chapter titled 'The Pitfalls of National Consciousness'. Both texts are clearly united in their lament of the curtailment of democracy in postcolonial Africa. For how else does a party and

[18] Pepetela, op cit., p. 79.
[19] Ibid., p. 79.

its leadership connect with the people by whose commitment, involvement and support it gained power and on whose behalf it claims power? Through a one way command structure? Pepetela seems to reject this.

As important is the obvious contradictions between a party of the working class and peasantry and its leadership composed almost entirely of middle-class intellectuals. Fearless argues that given the nature of cultural underdevelopment of a former colonial society, the party that leads the national movement is itself led by cadres who are themselves not workers and peasants although their parents may have been so. Who takes power in a postcolonial state was then a small group representing or seeking to represent the proletariat. Any degree of cultural and intellectual development of a worker who attains to positions of leadership necessarily takes him away from the very class that made him. Fearless claims that he is not against intellectuals and he in fact warns against anti-intellectualism in the party and society:

> What I am against is the principle of saying that a Party controlled by intellectuals is controlled by the proletariat. Because it is not true. This is the first lie, then come the others. It should be said that the Party is controlled by revolutionary intellectuals, who are trying to make policy in favour of the proletariat. But it begins with lying to the people, who see clearly that they control neither the Party nor the State and it is the beginning of mistrust, which is followed by demobilization.[20]

The cure for this would seem to lie in what Fanon also keeps on emphasising: that the middle-class intellectuals must never forget that they are either in the service of imperialism or of the people. Consciousness of the sovereignty of the people is the only way of seriously safeguarding against the corrupting tendencies inherent in holding power over others. The question

[20] Ibid., pp. 80-81.

then becomes one of finding ways of centering democracy among the party and the people and society as a whole rather than one of turning democratic centralism into a religious dogma.

One of the questions not adequately addressed in the narrative is that of the male and female in the national liberation struggle. Most precolonial African societies were patriarchal. The very existence of polygamy without a corresponding possibility for women, the fact that women never inherited land and property, and that the highest councils of power were occupied by men, would all indicate the subordination of women as a whole to men as a whole. In a communal society, the very negative effects of patriarchy may not have been too protruding a barrier in economic and political and military existence and development of that society. Many African societies were highly organised with councils of leadership for nearly every sector and age and sex. Even in a polygamous household, the woman was usually the head of her immediate household. She controlled the economic resources that were directly under her household. The man who would also have his own property would then act as the formal head of semi-autonomous domestic realms. But the real and potentially negative tendencies of patriarchy were reinforced by colonial capitalism. By taking away land, by turning men and women into wage earners, by taking away the power to organise, colonialism literally upset the internal balance of forces to the detriment of all, but women and children mostly. The African woman came under double patriarchy: the remnants of precapitalist feudal and customary traditions and the machismo of the entire colonial system. The frustrations of the work place at the factory or at the plantation, were often settled at home. Homes were anyway broken up with police raids even into people's private homes. In the cities, men were often forbidden to bring their wives and children into their work camps with prostitution replacing legalised marriages. Prostitution becomes a kind of polyandry with one woman available to more than one man with money as the mediator in the distribution of sexual favours. Colonial racism was also built on the assumption that woman, white or black, was property; and hence all those elaborate laws meant to bar African male access to white women but facilitating white male access to any black woman. In this way the colonial capitalist system distorts the entire relationship between male and female.

A national liberation struggle has to deal with this aspect. It is a subject hardly ever dealt with, because there are no easy answers, and yet one that desperately calls for thorough discussions at all the levels of the national movement and the party that heads it. One of the weaknesses in the narrative is the raising of the hope for a discussion of this aspect through the introduction of Ondine, and having an entire section named after her, but this is not the question that is addressed through her introduction. Ondine in fact simply becomes a sex object, almost a sexual measure of the prowess of those involved in the struggle. Simply put, which male can best satisfy her? A few other women appear although they are not at the centre of the narrative and the relationships of the central characters. Theory for instance thinks a great deal of the woman, Manuela, who he had to give up for politics and the guerrilla camp. Are they two alternatives? She is after all also living in a colonial society and she is subject to its contradictions. Singly or together they would have had to deal with the colonial question. Commander Fearless who originally was a seminarian escapes from the contradictions of a religious life under colonial racism by taking on a woman: 'It was with a mixture of holy terror, carnal delight and joyous vengeance that I had my first woman'.[21] Women then seem to function as the sexual means of men finding themselves politically. It is not that sex and sexual desires are not significant in the struggle. Or that

---

[21] Ibid., p. 21. '…a servant girl who provided relief for seminarists and, who knows, some of the fathers.'

they do not affect the course of history. Matters of the heart and sex can in fact cause tension in any group as much as matters of the mind. But a female, like a male, is more than her sexual organs and the palpitations of her heart. It is this significant silence over the question of women inside the movement that mars the unity of the narrative. Are there no women guerrillas? Would their presence and active participation in the Mayombe camp have altered the terms of the debates about nationalism, democracy and socialism? The issues of violence, language, racism and ethnicity? In what way? These questions arise as 'sins' of omission and especially so since many other issues are in fact brought into the picture. The loneliness of the leader: the person who has to make the final decision. Or the role of art and the artist in the national movement.

Can a narrative in which there is so much debate and discussions lay claim to art? The question can really only arise from an assumption that art has nothing to do with politics or with the weighty issues of our daily living. But really art has never been anything else but a way of organising our experience of history and society into a form that makes us see and feel more intensely. Art at its best appeals to both the heart and the head. It is not the subject matter of art that makes art but rather the organisation of that material into significant forms through language or paint or the chisel to create shape, balance, rhythm, force, movement and direction. It is when the material outweighs the form that the reader or the spectator feels the protrusions of the unwanted and therefore of the unstatisfying. It is difficult to discuss the use of language in *Mayombe* since the text being used is a translation. But it is possible to discuss the form. Pepetela has chosen multiple narrative voices and therefore viewpoints. He uses a combination of the more apparently objective voice of the omnipresent third person narrator and the 'I' narrative voices. The 'I' narrative voices function as confessional in a diary and give form to interiority of the different characters. The confessional form allows the freedom of thought of the various characters since in a confessional or in a diary anything goes. But they also function as correctives of biases in the voice of the omnipresent narrator. It also saves the omnipresent voice from dwelling too much within the interior of the characters. Together the various confessional narrative voices function as a chorus. They also enable the writer to cover the territorial and the historical landscape of Angola without departing from the vantage point of Mayombe, the theatre of the action in the present.

Pepetela has also chosen just a few significant actions around which to weave the narrative. In between, the waiting for the anticipated next action are lulls that allow characters to engage in various debates and discussions without making the reader feel that they are forced since they arise logically in the context of waiting. After all war, any war, is not fighting all the time. The actors are all in the struggle for the seizure of political power and it would be a strange group of active fighters for freedom who did not debate and discuss issues of war and peace and power. There is a kind of unity of time and place that gives the narrative as a whole significant form through which we can meaningfully look at how the content of the political struggle unfolds. The only section that tends to break the unity is that of Ondine. First it forces the narrative to leave Mayombe for a time. But the drama outside Mayombe, though it has an impact on what eventually transpires and gives us more information about the main actors, functions more like a digression rather than an integral part of the logic of the action in Mayombe itself.

Nevertheless *Mayombe* remains one of the most important narratives of the national consciousness focusing as it does on some of the great issues of the twentieth century: nationalism, democracy and socialism in war and peace.

Orature, Class Struggle & Nationalism

Vieira's *Luuanda*
& *The Real Life of Domingos Xavier*

José Luandino Vieira *Luuanda*
   (Translated from the Portuguese by Tamara L. Bender and
   Donna S. Hill; London: Heinemann AWS 222 1980)

Luuanda (Luuanda: ABC 1964; Brazil:1965; Lisboa: Edições 70
   1974)

—— *The Real Life of Domingos Xavier* (Translated from the
   Portuguese by Michael Wolfers; London: Heinemann AWS
   202 1978)

A Vida Verdadeira de Domingos Xavier (Lisboa: Edições 70 1974)

Vieira is another example of a writer whose life and letters cannot be divorced from politics. His writing arises from and also
draws on his own active involvement in the struggles for national
liberation. He is most certainly a good representative of the
hundreds of Angolans forced into prisons and exile because
of their involvement in MPLA and their commitment to social
change.

Born in 1935, he began working at the age of 15. He was
arrested in 1961 after MPLA had launched its armed struggle
against Portuguese colonialism with its attack on Luuanda
prisons and police posts in February the same year. He was
imprisoned on charges of distributing 'subversive literature' and
spent eight of the eleven years of his prison life, 1961-1972,

in Tarrafal prison in the Cape Verde islands where political prisoners opposed to Portuguese colonialism were sent. He was released in 1972, on conditional parole, and then exiled to Lisbon. He returned to Angola, in January 1975, after a military coup toppled the repressive Portuguese dictatorship. The same year, that is on 10 November 1975, Angola became independent under the leadership of Agostinho Neto and MPLA, bringing to an end four centuries of Portuguese colonial occupation of Angola. Among Vieira's most celebrated books were *Luuanda*, a collection of three short stories, and *The Real Life of Domingos Xavier*.

Luuanda

Luuanda has an interesting publishing history paralleling that of the author, if not actually rivalling it. The first edition came out in 1964. In 1965 it was awarded the Grand Prize for fiction by the Portuguese Writers Society. Within a few weeks of the award, the Portuguese secret police, raided the society's headquarters in Lisbon, physically wrecked the offices and closed the society down. *Luuanda* was banned from legal circulation. A clandestine edition published in Brazil in 1965 circulated underground in both Portugal and Angola. In 1972, soon after the author's release, the second legitimate edition of *Luuanda*, was brought out and it was banned for a second time. So it was only after the April 1974 military coup which overthrew the fascist Portuguese regime, that a third edition of *Luuanda* was reissued.

A marked feature of this collection is the writer's exploitation of orature. This is important because, in a colonial dictatorship, it is the voices of the peasant and the largely illiterate urban poor which are silenced. By drawing on orature Vieira is drawing on what is officially and in practice driven underground and so he is giving voice to silence. In the stories what one hears is the voice of the peasant and the tone of an African language. 'My intent in these narratives,' he himself has explained, as quoted in the translator's preface to the 1980 Heinemann edition of the book, 'was to take their structure from the oral tradition, employing the stylistic and linguistic characteristics of the popular oral language so that the tales themselves could be told aloud…' (p. vii).

The Kimbundu word for story is *musoso*, a moral story, allegory, fable, narrative or tale. All three stories are described as tales. This feature is easily the most recognisable in the opening and closing of the second and third tales. The tone at the beginning of 'The Tale of The Thief and The Parrot' is that of traditional narrator, probably at a fireside, plunging into a story, in a conversational manner: 'A certain Domelino dos Reis, Dosreis to his friends and ex-Lóló to the girls, was living with his wife and two children in the Sambizanga *musseque'* (p. 32). Or the opening of 'The Tale of The Hen and The Egg': 'The tale of the hen and the egg happened in the *musseque* of Sambizanga, in this our land of Luanda' (p. 88).

The endings of both these narratives are even more definite in their tone of a traditional story-telling. In 'The Tale of The Thief and The Parrot': 'So that's my tale. If it's pretty or if it's ugly, only those who can read can say. But I swear that's how they told it and I won't let anyone doubt [my characters].... And that's the truth, even if none of it ever happened' (p. 86).

The unfolding of the stories have all the sudden, abrupt twists, and digressions of a conversational narrative. An important element of the oral story is recurring phrases usually in the form of a song that serves to punctuate the narrative and to make it easier for the listeners to follow. There are also dramatic elements, sometimes in the form of mimes. A good example of this is in the 'The Tale of The Hen and The Egg' when the children, Xico and Beto, try to demonstrate their claims that Cabiri the hen in dispute, is actually talking and that they can understand what it is saying:

> Suddenly Beto left his hiding place in the *mandioqueira* tree and said before Xico could even begin. 'The hen talks like this, Grandma:
>
> > 'Ngëxile kua ngana Zefa
> > Ngala ngó ku kakela
> > Ká...ká...ká..kakela, kakela...'
>
> And then Xico, with his squeaky voice, went over to his friend and the two of them began to sing just like Cabiri who became all confused, wriggling her head, hearing the other hen but not seeing it:
>
> > '...ngëjile kua ngana Bina
> > Ala kiá ku kuata
> > kua...kua...kua...kuata, kuata!'
>
> And they began to pretend they were hens pecking at the corn on the ground. Grandma scolded them to be quiet. *Nga* Zefa started to chase after Beto and the two friends went running out of the yard. (p. 95-6)

The traditional story and its format fits into the views of art discussed within 'The Tale of The Thief and The Parrot'. The discussion comes in as part of the privileged role of the teller who is allowed to interrupt the narrative to point out a moral or make any necessary observation or digression. In this case the fictional voice, a kind of narrator-within-a-narrator, is that of Xico Futa, the sympathetic policeman. He asks:

> Can people really know, for sure, how something started, where it started, why, what for, who by? Really know what was going on in the heart of the person who starts confusions, looks for them, or undoes or ruins conversations? Or is it impossible to grab on to the beginning of things in life, when you get to that beginning you

see after all that same beginning was the end of another beginning
and then, if you go on like this, backwards and forwards, you see
that the thread of life can't be broken, even if it is rotten at some
point, it always mends itself at another point, it grows, it strays,
flees, advances, turns, stops, disappears, appears.' (pp. 43-4)

So for a narrator, the choice of a beginning is really an arbitrary
act. Everything is connected:

The thread of life that shows the why, the how of arguments, even
if it is rotten, doesn't break. Pulling it, fixing it, you always find
a beginning at some point, even if this beginning is the end of
another beginning. (p. 44)

The artistic creative process is identified with that of life itself in
the image of a cashew tree whose real roots one can never reach.
Life is rich, varied, continuous and one cannot kill it. In the same
way one cannot kill art. But just as one can never get at the roots
of life, at the beginning of life, at the end of life, so if one is
telling things of life, one has to arbitrarily choose a beginning.
Says Xico Futa: 'a beginning must be chosen' (p. 46). But what
one narrates is only a slice of life, part of a continuum.

This is the artistic method which Vieira has chosen. He takes
a slice of life, an episode, explores it in its particularity and
generality. The particular has to be seen as part of something else,
just as art has to be seen as part of life. Hence for instance one is
always being made aware of other things happening, out there, in
the larger society. One is aware of police stations, armed soldiers
prowling about in the streets, and above all, the overwhelming
presence of prison and its environments of armed warders and
political prisoners. The inner life is also connected to the outer:
we are made aware of the drama going on inside each character
even as they interact in the action of the present. Violence is in
the air; but so is the resistance which is associated with the land,
the rains, nature, life!

A discussion of the three stories, 'Grandma Xixi and Her Grandson Zeca Santos', 'The Tale of The Thief and The Parrot', and 'The Tale of The Hen and The Egg', should bring out more clearly Vieira's use of orality in a literary work that so well carries voices of resistance. The three stories are set in a *musseque*. In the glossary we are told that this Kimbundu word originated from the phrase *ngoloia mu seke* (I'm going where the earth is clay-like). *Seke* designated the coarse rust-colored sand good for growing manioc which could be found throughout the city of Luanda. As more and more people came to the capital, the manioc crops disappeared and in their place there sprung up thousands of shanties which sheltered these poor newcomers to the city (p.115).

So, up to independence, *musseque* implied the ghetto. Already in the setting of the story is the colonial irony: the earth which used to be the basis of plenty, yielding life, yields only poverty and squalor. Thus if, in the days of yore, it had rained this would have been the sign of life beginning. But now

> By noon the rain became lighter even though the sky was still ugly and sneering, all black with clouds. The *musseque* seemed like a village floating in the middle of a lagoon, with canals made by rain and the shanties invaded by the red, dirty water rushing towards the tar roads Downtown or stubbornly staying behind to make muddy pools for mosquitoes and noisy frogs. Some of the shanties had fallen down and the people, not wanting to drown, were outside them with the few things they could save. Beneath the grey sunless sky only the blades of grass were shining a prettier colour, their washed green heads peeking out from the pools of water. (p. 3)

The story of 'Grandma Xixi and Her Grandson Zeca Santos' could be described as the loneliness of a jobseeker in a colonial society. He says: 'Every day I go out for work. Downtown I walk and walk and walk – and there is nothing! Not even in the *musseque...*' (p.4). Hunger and violence stalk the jobseeker. The repetitiveness of hunger, no food, no money, no job, is oppressive in its insistence that this was the normal condition of life in colonial Angola. Twice when he goes to look for work he is actually beaten or chased away particularly when the potential employers discover his connection with the political prisoners. He comes from Catete where Agostinho Neto was born and where there were many recruits into MPLA. So there is a political reason for his unemployment and for the hunger. It is the colonial politics of oppression and underdevelopment that create unemployment and hunger. The fact that he fails to get jobs because of his connection with the leadership of the political movement is a reminder that there is resistance going on out there.

The colonial social landscape is bleak. It is one of loneliness perhaps best expressed in Grandma's helplessness to come to the aid of the child she so loves. She cannot feed herself; she cannot feed him. It is also seen in the shame that seizes Zeca for even desiring to live. Zeca is feeling ashamed within himself for simply desiring those things that any young person his age would desire. Life for the poor in colonial Angola is a bleak landscape of unfulfilled desires and hopes and hunger for the ordinary means of survival. There is no dignity in poverty but the poor have dignity. They have their fleeting moments of triumph, of memory, of dreams, of fantasies, like Grandma's images of herself as Madame Cecilia with a decent house in decent surroundings. There is also Zeca's memory of his triumph over the arrogant more well to do João Rosa, or moments of love and tenderness like when he is with Delfina, or moments of pride like when he refuses food that he desperately needs and claims that he has already eaten. These moments point to the possibilities of life and they sustain him helping him to cling to a dignity continuously undermined by hunger and the helplessness of a jobless jobseeker and the spectre of even more hunger. But the greatest moments of all are those of solidarity best seen in the contact between Grandma Xixi and Zeca. It is as if they only have themselves. The poor have only their solidarity, and in a way, this is their greatest asset. Solidarity of the oppressed is seen as of the highest moral good and hence in the other stories and certainly in *The Real Life of Domingos Xavier*, the biggest crime a person can commit would be for him go against the people, to betray the trust of a group.

'The Tale of The Thief and The Parrot' tells the story of Garrido Kam'tuta, crippled in one leg from paralysis and his unrequited love for Inácia Domingos, a young girl who dreams of a middle-class life of luxury. Part of her is attracted to him, his words enlarge her imagination, but when he criticises her for thinking only about clothes and houses and material things as defined by the white community, she turns against him and find words and actions to hurt him. Garrido Kam'tuta is constantly being humiliated by Inácia and even by a parrot that has been taught words to mock at him. That a mere parrot should mock at him even though it is only parroting words of the master, is too much for him and he decides to fight back. He will steal the parrot, even kill it, choke it to death. Kam'tuta gathers courage to steal the parrot but he is unwittingly betrayed by Dosreis to the police. Dosreis has been arrested for stealing some ducks to feed his wife and two kids and he wrongly suspects Garrido Kam'tuta of having told on him. What of course emerges is the courage of the two men, one a boy, the other elderly, but both living under the indignity and humiliations of poverty. Both fight back for their dignity and self-esteem, and in the process, express resistance in their different ways. When Lomelino dos Reis, Dosreis to his friends, is arrested and taken to the police station, he takes great exception to the police calling him a bandit. And when Zuzé, one of the policemen knocks him down, Dosreis fights back, for, as he argues, he may be in rags, but he is human, with human needs and desires. He would not allow anybody, not even the police, to push him around without his fighting back. In the same way, Kam'tuta who has been humiliated by everybody is virtually transformed when he decides to fight back, to stand up to life and not surrender. When he stands up to one of the able-bodied boys, João Miguel, we are told that 'There in the night Garrido Kam'tuta grew straight, no longer the lopsided boy with his head always down, hiding in every corner, running from the *monas* who chased after him with insults' (p. 69). Human dignity emerges precisely from the decision to fight back, to stand up to life with whatever ounce of human energy one possesses. But once again, as in the story of Grandama Xixi, it is the solidarity among the wretched of the earth that is seen as among the highest of moral values. What hurts Kam'tuta, even more than the fact of being betrayed to the police by Dosreis, is the knowledge that the betrayal was based on Dosreis' assumption that Kam'tuta had squealed to the police. Kam'tuta keeps on asking himself, how could people whom he had thought of as friends, as neighbours, how could they ever think of him in those terms? And the story ends with the two prisoners rediscovering their unity, their sense of human solidarity even under the harsh conditions of their social being.

Similar themes run through the third story: 'The Tale of The Hen and The Egg'. The story is very simple: it is a dispute as to who has the right to Cabiri, the hen. The hen actually belongs to *Nga* Zefa. But she is always feeding in Bina's yard. So when she lays an egg in Bina's yard, to whom does the egg really belong? To Bina who actually feeds the chicken that bore the egg or to Zefa who owns the body of the chicken but hardly ever feeds it? To complicate matters, Bina is pregnant and she clearly needs the egg for the proteins. Many people come onto the scene and try and settle the dispute; the neighbours, a cleric from the Catholic church, the landlord, a student of law, the tax collector and they all have their different interpretations depending largely on their class background and social status. Behind the mask of oral simplicity, the story raises basic questions about the ownership of property. Who owns the land? Capital? Who has the right to what capital produces? Labour produces? What about use? Should it be based solely on ownership and possession or also on need? Other questions arise from this: for instance the relationship between law and justice. Law, colonial law in particular, or its interpretation emerges as means of mystifying the realities of oppression and resistance. Education too. Eventually, the question of the people, ordinary people, and their capacity to run their own affairs: are they capable of judging matters that concern their lives? In fact when the people stop deferring to external authority and they rely on their own collective sense, they are shown as settling the case through discussions and they arrive at the position of putting human needs at the forefront. Justice for the people then consists in meeting human needs. Without departing from the structure and format of an oral tale, Vieira manages to show clearly the class basis of actions and value judgements in class and race structured societies.

The story also affirms another important value in all the stories: discussion, arguments, debates, disagreements as the basis of truth. The story of the hen and the egg is like one continuous indaba, baraza, neighbourhood assemblies of a people's government. It also brings back the words of Xico Futa the narrator in the story of the parrot:

> People talk, the ones who are in the arguments, who suffer through these affairs, these confusions, they tell, and right there, right then, when some confusion happens, each one tells his truth and if they

go on talking and disputing, the truth begins to bear fruit, finally it becomes a full basket of truth and a basket of lies, because a lie is already a time of truth or its very opposite. (p. 44)

In the preliminary draft of his novel, *Au Bonheur des Dames*, the nineteenth-century French novelist, Emile Zola wrote: '*Je veux faire le poème de l'activité moderne.*' In his stories, using the artistic forms of the Angolan peasantry, José Luandino Vieira has done what Emile Zola tried to do: in his case write poems out of the ordinary existence and struggles of the peasant and the urban poor. Write poems in celebration of the solidarity of the wretched of the earth.

The Real Life of Domingos Xavier

Solidarity as both a political act and a moral value is the main theme celebrated in his novel, *The Real Life of Domingos Xavier.* Once again the narrative is deceptively simple. Domingos Xavier, a tractor driver, arrested by the Portuguese secret police, is taken to Luuanda prison, where he is tortured and eventually killed without having given any information about the liberation movement of which he is a member. But woven around this event is an elaborate celebration of Angolan nationalism conceived once again in the images of the land, the waters, the languages, the orature, and the actions of the people of Angola. Dominating the narrative is the prison as the symbol and reality of the oppressive machinery of the colonial state. The prison swallows many sons and daughters of Angola, some are killed without their identities ever being disclosed. But the movement has taken measures to counteract the lies. To the colonial state's misinformation system, its culture of literacy that writes lies through false police reports and records, the nationalists have countered with an elaborate oral communication system. A combination of the oral fax, network, telegraph is seen at work in how Domingos Xavier's presence in the Luuanda prison is quickly communicated; how in fact the unknown becomes known; and the dead become resurrected in the people's collective memory and life.

Zito, a young boy, playing outside the walls of the prison is among the first to see the prisoner as the police bring him in. He communicates this to his grandfather, Old Petelo, who in turn takes the news to Chico, then Chico to Mussunda all the way back to Domingos' village and the community where they discover his name and therefore identity, thus transforming him from an unknown prisoner to Domingos Xavier, a tractor driver, Maria's husband and a father and a member of the movement. The connection between the historical event and the fictional event are obvious. It becomes literally a chain of human contacts each person putting their trust in the next link in the network of resistance. It is a political network of trust and discipline and solidarity.

This solidarity is manifested for instance in the acts of Mama Zefa in support of Maria, Domingos' wife, and their baby, Basty. It is that solidarity that gives Maria the strength to face the various colonial police posts, literally following in the footsteps of her husband all the way to Luuanda prison where her presence is also noted by Zito. In Luuanda she gets similar support from Mama Terry and other women. The solidarity extends to inside the walls of the prison. And not surprisingly the women, even the ones she does not know, are there with her when finally she gets intimations about her husband's death. We are told that the women brushed down her cloths, helped her tie her baby on her back and they stayed talking. But each knew that any one of them could be the victim of the loss of a spouse at the hands of the Salazar's secret police. The women feel the death of Domingos as a collective loss.

No sooner is Domingos shut in his cell than he gets a note asking him not to tell anything. They knew nothing. The note which is signed by Timothy, gives him tremendous strength despite his swollen body: 'how good it was to know that there was a *companheiro* nearby, how good it was to feel the warmth of solidarity!' Domingos monologues to himself. The act makes him feel even more strongly 'the duty not to betray the friends who trusted him, not betray to his land' (p. 36). The sense of oneness in the struggle is dramatised in the death scene. From all corners of the prison, the people come to sit in silence round the dying brother, supporting him in whatever they can, little acts of human sympathy that speak resistance for miles.

Heroism consists in whatever acts a person can undertake to keep alive and secret the links that bind them. So throughout the interrogation, there is only one phrase that keeps on coming out of Domingos' tortured body: 'I don't know' or a variation of that. And it is the refrain, I am not telling, I am not telling, that echoes in Maria's heart. And it is this act of not telling the secrets of his people that is identified with heroism and nationalism: '... our brother carried himself like a man, he did not tell the secrets of his people, he did not sell himself. We are not going to weep any more for his death because, ...' and here they address him directly as if he is present among them, 'Domingos Antonio Xavier, you begin today your real life in the hearts of the Angolan people...' (p. 84).

Vieira makes it clear in the narrative that Angolan nationalism is not spontaneous simply because one is born on Angolan soil and lives in the ghetto. It develops through taking acts against the colonialism. A person comes to it through his life's experience, and through political education in discussions. Although Angola is a under a white Portuguese colonial dictatorship that practises racism all the way, the narrative stresses the primacy of class, class ideology, consciousness and solidarity. Domingos is introduced to the movement. So is Chico. Chico used to love dancing to the exclusion of almost everything until he meets Mussunda, the tailor. Before he had always believed that the rich provided work, money and charity to the poor. In other words colonial capitalism was for the good of the likes of him. It is Mussunda who explains to him that if the money of the rich was lying idle, it would not yield anything, capital needed labour to yield anything. Mussunda's discussions opened his eyes and showed him that behind the masks of black, white and mulatto, was the reality of the rich and the poor. He comes to realise more keenly what in essence he already knew: that justice in a colonial society is justice for the bosses who happen to be white but bosses all the same. Political action on behalf of change also changes Chico so that he becomes much more than a good dancer. He was now a political activist, Gramsci's organic intellectual, who could also dance well.

In this novel, like in the stories in *Luuanda*, the Angolan land-scape and the sky are active. Chico emerging from depressing memories of racist insults he has just witnessed and memories of many more in the past, is restored to his lively spirits by 'The murmuring sound of the sea, brushing along the sand… It brought too, on its journey, the good smell of the Angolan coast…' (p. 31). A depressed Maria is woken up to her commit-ment to find her husband by the blue sky and the sun and the people all mixed up in her mind to give her a sense of calm. But nature can also become angry as when torrents of rain destroy people's houses. While in prison, images of waters of Angola fill Domingos' thoughts cushioning him against the physical pain from the police beatings. And at night when the moonlight penetrates into his cell, he felt that it was the blue sky and the moon of his land that watched over him. And when he closes his eyes to sleep, he feels Kuanza river run into the moonlight, 'roaring and angry or tame and gentle, a broad sea without waves' (p.17). Even the power of sleep is identified with the power of

Kuanza river: like Kuanza nothing withstood it. 'Stretched out, he let himself float on the river of his childhood, of the plateau which had witnessed his birth' (p. 18). The sounds and memories of Kuanza river accompany him on the day he is killed:

> Outside, stars shone over the hot countryside and a fresh wind travelled through the night and brought the message of life within the walls. Domingos Xavier was not going to betray that life. He could still think and he felt himself floating on the green waters of the river which had witnessed his birth and which was carrying him out to sea. (p. 67)

Throughout the narrative, it is the people's irrepressible sense of life that is really the essence of the resistance. It is this sense of life that colonialism is out to destroy and in the case of Angola had been out to destroy for the last four hundred years. But this life rooted in the land and their culture refuses to die out. It asserts itself through their songs and dances. Thus when the prisoners gather around Domingos' body, they finally break out into a song:

> And the chorus which followed vaulted the prison walls and, swift as the fresh wind of dawn, filled all the white night of the township. And not all the whips of all the *cipaios* sent into the prison could silence the prisoners before daybreak. (p. 69)

The Saturday dance at Mussunda's house was welcome to the people because they knew that it meant:

> Angolan music, Angolan food, everything! It meant Brazilian music and Cuban as well, the people, music of Bahia and merengue! And none of that canned music from the radio, not that. A live group, the people's group, like the Ngola, on this night. (p. 77)

Resistance against oppression is really a celebration of life. The colonial state would like to 'stamp out people's stubborn joy' and that's why despite the fact that people are dying in prison, those outside continue to dance and sing for they argue that they must never allow the police state to celebrate their death and silence. They had to dance and sing as an expression of the people's vitality and enjoyment of life, which could not be suppressed even by the arrests and killings.

There is a way in which both art and life imitate one another. MPLA launched its armed struggle with an attack on Luuanda prisons at dawn in February 1961. Luandino Vieira finished his narrative on 10 November 1961. On 1 December 1968, a boy aged 12, was beaten to death by Portuguese soldiers for refusing to reveal the location of his school and an MPLA detachment. Today the date is celebrated as Pioneer's Day in Angola. But the date and the death had already been celebrated, and it continues to be celebrated in Luandino Vieira's narrative. Domingos Xavier represents all the unknown and known soldiers of the revolution in Angola, Africa and the World.

Writing a National Agender
Patriarchy as Domestic Colonialism
in Tsitsi Dangarembga's *Nervous Conditions*

Tsitsi Dangarembga *Nervous Conditions.*
  (London: The Women's Press 1988/Olympia, WA: Seal
  Press 1989; republished 2004: Banbury: Ayebia Publishing/
  Boulder, CO: Lynne Rienner Publishers)

In the Preface to Frantz Fanon's *The Wretched of the Earth*, Jean-Paul Sartre argues that the European bourgeoisie set up to manufacture, in Africa, Asia, and South America, their native counterparts. He does not, as it is so often the case, attach too much significance to the differences in the cultural policies of the different colonising powers, the assimilisionism of the French and the pragmatism of the British, for instance. The methods and the ends are essentially the same:

> They picked out promising adolescents; they branded them, as with a red-hot iron, with the principles of western culture; they stuffed their mouths full with high-sounding phrases, grand glutinous words that stuck to the teeth. After a short stay in the mother country they were sent home, whitewashed.[1]

These Graeco-Latin Africans as he calls them would become mere echoes of Europe and they would lead, as Fanon explains when he talks about varieties of violence in a colonial system,

[1] Jean-Paul Sartre, Preface to Frantz Fanon *The Wretched of the Earth* (New York: The Grove Edition 1991, p. 7).

a life of nervous conditions.[2] An echo is precisely an echo and never a reproduction of the original under new conditions. What is the impact of these Graeco-Latin Africans when they are in positions of power? How do they impact the population and particularly the women of all classes? And what should women do about it? These and more are the questions that the Zimbabwean writer Tsitsi Dangarembga tries to explore in her narrative *Nervous Conditions*. She is of that new generation of poets and writers committed to explaining that European bourgeois values and the true lives of the working people of Africa are in opposition. Even the Graeco-Latin Africans, do not become so, totally, they are simply bad copies of the original. The nervous conditions arise from the fact that the recipients of these Western bourgeois values, whose genesis and growth are permeated through and through by racism, can neither 'reject them completely nor yet assimilate them'.

The narrative, in the first person singular, is, on the surface, the story of a girl coming of age in Zimbabwe, then Rhodesia, during the era of UDI and the anti-colonial guerrilla war. The fictional-I-narrator, Tambudzai, tells us that her brother, Nhamo, dies in 1968 when she is thirteen. She was born in 1955. She is therefore ten when her uncle Babamukuru returns from England in 1965. Historically, what is known as UDI (Unilateral Declaration of Independence), took place on 11 November 1965. But by then ZANLA and ZAPLA guerrillas had already entered the country, striking significant blows and psychological victories in the battles of Sinoia in 1966,[3] and at Wankie game reserve in July 1967. Zimbabwe becomes independent in April 1980.

---

[2] Ibid., p.17: 'The status of "native" is a nervous condition...'

[3] David Martin and Phyllis Johnson *The Struggle for Zimbabwe* (London: Faber 1981), pp. 9-10. At the battle of Sinoia seven of the guerrillas, part of a group of twenty one, 'died in a fierce encounter with the Rhodesian troops backed by helicopter gunships. It was the deepest penetration into Rhodesia in this phase of the war by any guerilla group and today ZANU marks 28 April as Chimurenga Day, the official start of the war.'

So Tambudzai's coming of age takes place during the year of struggle and therefore parallels Zimbabwe's own coming of age. In the narrative the armed struggle is not foregrounded. There are references to it like when we are told that Nyasha differs from her father over the fact, *inter alia*, that he calls freedom fighters terrorists. But by fixing the year 1965 as marking the return of Babamukuru to Rhodesia and hence the beginnings of the events that were to lead to the writing of this personal narrative, the author and the text invite an awareness of the larger social and political narrative unfolding in the mountains and forests and urban centres. The action of the novel is largely limited to the domestic and personal planes. Here patriarchy rules supreme. Its authority, though, unfolds in a colonial space. It is a colonised patriarchy. There is a connection between the domestic and the political spheres. The patriarch, Babamukuru, and the Mission, from which he derives much of his authority, are to the domestic realm what Zimbabwe as a whole is to the colonial state and the colonising country. Thus while the larger political sphere is kept strictly in the background, its effects permeate the domestic scene that mirrors it.

The action of the novel is deceptively simple. It is an intellectual and emotional autobiography – the coming of age of the head and the heart so to speak – describing, in the process, the educational journey that eventually leads the fictional narrator to write this story. The writing of the story itself – like the larger narrative being written in the landscape of Zimbabwean geography and history is itself integral to the growing up process, and is a preliminary summation of her life before the next stage. She sees this period of what she calls 'that process of expansion'[4]

---

[4] Tsitsi Dangarembga *Nervous Conditions* (The Seal Press Edition, 1989). First published in the UK by The Women's Press 1988, Seal Press (WA) 1989, and republished and reset by Ayebia Clarke Publishing 2004 with Lynne Rienner Publishers (CO). Page references are given to both editions, pp. 203/208.

as containing all the events 'that put me in a position to write this account'[5]. The account is of a poor African girl and her struggle for education and in that sense it is every poor girl's story in Africa and the world. She interacts with mainly two groups, male and female, whose actions on each other symbolise the struggle a woman has to go through in a patriarchal colonial system.

The male group consists of her uncle, Babamukuru, educated in South Africa, Britain and now the African headmaster of a mission school; her own father, Jeremiah, eternally grateful to his brother; and her older brother, Nhamo, who dies the death of the spirit long before he dies that of the flesh. The female group consists of her mother, who describes women of her class as carrying three burdens of class, race and gender, what she calls the poverty of blackness and the weight of her womanhood;[6] Maiguru, Babamukuru's wife, whose education is buried under the weight of her wifeliness; Lucia, her mother's sister, who rejects wifeliness as defined by patriarchy; and Nyasha who rebels against the colonised authority of the African male. There are a few other minor African characters who hover around but they reflect more or less the characteristics of the two groups. There are also the whites who are not foregrounded but whose overwhelming presence is felt all around like an inescapable malevolence that somehow runs their lives or determines the parameters of space and time within which their lives will be played out. The armed struggle is also in the background, a struggle for liberation, against which the woman-man relationships of inequality, of dominance and subjugation, has to be seen.

The unequal relationship between male and female in both feudal and colonial societies is symbolised by Tsitsi Tambudzai and

[5]   Ibid., p. 1/1.
[6]   Ibid., p. 16/16. She articulates this graphically: 'This business of womanhood is a heavy burden…. How could it not be? Aren't we the ones who bear children? … And these days it is worse, with the poverty of blackness on one side and the weight of womanhood on the other.'

Nhamo and their chances of access to formal education. Being black and poor in a colonial society, they both have narrowed opportunities for schooling. But when money is available, it is automatically assumed and taken for granted that it is the boy and not the girl who must seize the chance. In other words their genders determine who goes to school under the limitations imposed by poverty. The question as to who is intellectually better placed to make use of the opportunity does not arise. But matters go deeper than the question of available opportunities. The male group is depicted as being actively opposed to her seizing whatever chances she has of advancing herself.

Nothing exemplifies better both the girl's determination and the patriarchy ganged up against her than the scene where she puts in a lot of work on her garden to grow corn which she hopes to sell and so raise money for school. She is then only eight years. Her brother steals the maize to give it away to friends in school. And when she finally manages to raise money in Umtali through the intervention of the kindly school teacher, Mr Matimba, and a chance encounter with Doris, a white woman, her father, Jeremiah, schemes to take it away from her, claiming the money really belongs to him by virtue of his having fathered her. It is more than just the question of greed. Her father wants her to remain trapped within her femininity. 'He did not like to see me overabsorbed in intellectual pursuits' the narrator comments and describes how Jeremiah becomes literally agitated whenever he finds her reading from old sheets of newspapers because he thinks that she is emulating her brother and 'that the things I read would fill my mind with impractical ideas, making me quite useless for the real tasks of feminine living.[7] Thus like colonial racism that not only gives whites wings with which to fly but finds it necessary to clip those of the blacks and literally tie their feet to the ground, here African maleness is not just

[7] Ibid., pp. 33/34.

satisfied with giving another male a chance, but must literally tie down the feminine to the hearth and subsistence agriculture. The male-female relationship here is depicted as reproducing that of the coloniser and the colonised: the coloniser feels threatened by the very thought that the other, through writing and reading, might entertain the wrong ideas. White settlers and the colonial state generally were hostile to African educational advancement; they might become part of those 'uppity niggers' who do not know their God-ordained place in a colonial universe. In a patriarchal universe, the woman should know and keep her place.

Tambudzai's chances of a real educational breakthrough comes about only through Nhamo's death and that is why the death of her brother is central to the narrative and to her development. 'It is unfortunate that there is no male child to take this duty, to take this job of raising the family from hunger and need,' says Babamukuru, as a preliminary to offering the opportunity to the only alternative available. Nhamo's invisibility is the beginning of her visibility. It explains the startling admission by the narrator that she was actually happy when her brother dies. But it is worth noting, as the narrative itself underlines, that she is sent to the mission to become what her brother was intended to become. Thus in terms of patriarchy she is to become a male for a time before marriage turns her into a woman again. 'this girl ...Tambudzai – must be given the opportunity to do what she can for the family before she goes into her husband's home'[8] Babamukuru pronounces. Thus as a potential provider of the family, a male destiny, she becomes an honorary male, at least for a time, because eventually she would fulfil her woman's destiny in marriage. But if Nhamo is the image of the future of Tambudzai, is she going to end up the same way, in a moral if not an actual physical death? The death of Nhamo and the departure of Tambudzai invite one of the central questions in

8   Ibid., both quotes, p. 56/56.

the narrative: the nature of Western education in general and colonial education in particular!

Thus if the novel dramatises the struggle of a girl for schooling, it also poses many questions about education in a colonial society for both men and women and it centres the title and Fanonistic critique of colonialism. What kind of education is Tambudzai going to get? Is Tambduzai going to be a Graeco-Latin African female? There are at least three ways of looking at the politics of education in the novel.

Education is perceived by the main actors, particularly the male, as an economic investment, a means of escape from the colonial circle of poverty. The recipients may not live the exact lifestyle of their white counterparts but certification gives them a better chance of doing better than their black neighbours. Babamukuru is the symbol of the successful product of this aspect of education. The narrator sees him as being different, the one who had not cringed under the weight of poverty. 'Boldly, Babamukuru had defied it. Through hard work and determination he had broken the evil wizard's spell.'[9] Through an education in Rhodesia and degrees from South African and British universities, and, of course, as the holder of a profession in a mission school, he now had 'Plenty of power. Plenty of Money. A lot of education. Plenty of everything.'[10] And Nhamo is sent to the mission to distinguish himself academically at least sufficiently so, that he 'would lift our branch of the family out of the squalor in which we were living.'[11]

Over and over again, directly and indirectly, it is made very clear to Tambudzai that she gets her chance at the mission school so that she might inherit this aspect of her brother, as a holder of an education that might turn her into a provider for the family;

[9] Ibid., p. 50/50.
[10] Ibid., p. 50/50.
[11] Ibid., p. 4/4.

a male destiny, at least for a time, before she fulfils her woman's destiny in marriage. Lest she remains in doubt about her future as mapped out for her, Babamukuru explains to her that the opportunity for mental improvement was only a means to material emancipation for the entire family and not an individual blessing. But most important is the fact that at the mission she would learn how to be a good woman, to learn proper femaleness and wifeliness.[12] While the key is material emancipation on the family's behalf there is a contradiction noted by the narrator, for to play the role of the male, even though in a temporary capacity, is to be freed from one aspect of the burden of womanhood, an unquestioning wifeliness, and would the genie so readily go back into the bottle afterwards?[13]

She never forgets the materialistic aspect of the great expectations. When she gets a scholarship to go to a convent school, she argues that whatever negative baggage she might have to carry, it was outweighed by the vision of one day being able to dress her sisters in pretty clothes and to feed her mother until she was plump and energetic once again. 'Money would do all this for me. With the ticket I would acquire attending the convent, I would

[12] Ibid., pp. 87-8/88-9. The sermon is worth quoting in length. 'As it turned out, Babamukuru had summoned me to make sure that I knew how lucky I was to have been given this opportunity for mental and eventually, through it, material emancipation. He pointed out that the blessing I had received was not an individual blessing but one that extended to all members of my less fortunate family, who would be able to depend on me in the future as they were now depending on him. Lastly, he explained, at the mission I would not only go to school but learn ways and habits that would make my parents proud of me. *I was an intelligent girl but I had also to develop into a good woman,* he said stressing both qualities equally and not seeing any contradiction in this.'

[13] African narratives are full of incidents where people are sent for formal learning in the colonial school with one hope, but who end up being involved in a mass of contradictions. The classic case is that in Achebe's *The Arrow of God* of Ezeulu sending Oduche to school so he could be his spy at the mission school, when Oduche comes back ready to kill the sacred python of the community. But similar sentiments are captured and discussed in Cheikh Hamidou Kane's novel *Ambiguous Adventure.* Similarly in Ngũgĩ's *The River Between!*

earn lots of it.'[14] Schooling was a means of acquiring a ticket to material well-being. Here she sounds very like an echo of both Nhamo and Babamukuru.

But education, particularly for the woman, is also seen as having the possibility of a different kind of emancipation, a spiritual emancipation, an awakening to a capacity to question, to formulate and articulate ideas about the world. It is not this aspect of education that Babamukuru has in mind when he talks to her but the narrator is very well aware of this possibility. She describes her transfer to the mission as the period of my reincarnation. She expects the era to be 'significantly profound and broadening in terms of adding wisdom to my nature, clarity to my vision, glamour to my person.' Indeed she plunges into books with a sense of tremendous gratitude to the authors 'for introducing me to places where reason and inclination were not at odds. It was a centripetal time, with me at the centre, everything gravitating towards me. It was a time of sublimation with me as the sublime.'[15]

Similarly Nyasha is depicted as wanting to understand the world around her and her place in it. She likes reading about politics and history and the Third World and liberation struggles, about what she calls real people and their real conditions. So she reads about South Africa, Palestine, Japan, the holocaust, the precolonial society, about UDI. And Lucia decides to go back to school – adult education – and it is clearly hinted that she does so because she wants to broaden her intellectual space. So that when Tambudzai, at the end of her life in the mission, earns a scholarship to the convent school and says that she was now about to take another step upwards in the direction of her

[14] Ibid., pp. 183/186.
[15] Ibid., pp. 92-3/94. In a significant number of narratives by women writers colonial education is not always seen in terms of disaster. There is a way in which it functions to free the female character from the negative burdens of irrelevant traditionalism. See Flora Nwapa *Efuru* and Mariama Bâ in *So Long a Letter*.

freedom, the word freedom has echoes that go well beyond the acquisition of economic benefits.

The first two aspects of education – as a means of economic emancipation on the behalf of the community, and as a means of spiritual emancipation – are contradicted by a third aspect: Education as a process of alienation from the self and the community. Before Nhamo has gone to the mission school he has, within himself, a very important thing: he is one with the family: 'we had been able to agree that although our squalor was brutal, it was uncompromisingly ours; that the burden of dispelling it was, as a result, ours too. But then something that he saw at the mission turned his mind to thinking that our homestead no longer had any claim upon him.'[16] Indeed even before he enters the mission, he is talking proudly of being educated into *not being Jeremiah's son*.[17] And at the end of the first year, he comes home physically changed for the better, '…but there was one terrible change. He had forgotten how to speak Shona.'[18] The changes in him are so remarkable that his mother thinks that 'someone on the mission was bewitching her son and was all for making an appointment with the [native spiritual] medium.'[19] Indeed his physical death is actually preceded by the spiritual death and that's why the mother, the only character without any spiritual corruption, can tell that her son is dead even before the news is broken to her. 'Why do you come all this way to tell me what I already know!', she tells Babamukuru. 'First you took his tongue so that he could not speak to me and now you have taken everything, taken everything for good…

[16] Ibid., p. 7/7.
[17] Ibid., p. 48/48. 'Babamukuru says I am so bright I must be taken away to a good school and be given a good chance in life. So I shall go and live with Babamukuru at the mission. I shall no longer be Jeremiah's son.' Those lines take us back to the observation of Jean-Paul Sartre on the practice of colonial education in his Preface to Fanon's *The Wretched of the Earth*.
[18] Ibid., pp. 52-3/52-3.
[19] Ibid., p. 53/53.

You and your education have killed my son.'[20]

Similarly, Nyasha and her brother Chido who have been educated in England are seen as hybrids: neither completely Zimbabwean nor completely English. Nyasha is partly saved by her thirst for knowledge. Through her readings and questions she has arrived at the conclusion that colonial education is a system of assimilation. Nyasha belongs to that category of the native elite who fight against being completely assimilated by the West and yet are indelibly marked and defined by it in the absence of a strong anchor in the culture of their people. In trying to find strength from within themselves, their mind becomes literally a battleground of conflicting tendencies and desires. It is like a long-term prisoner who can only escape into the prison yard of his jailers it being the only world he has known. Her father, Babamukuru, on the other hand, does not seem to be aware of any conflict. He is a complete echo of the colonising other. The essential nature of an echo is not altered by the reality against which it reproduces the sounds of the original voice. In his case the original voices are in Europe or in their white representatives at the colonial capital and at the mission. For him the Zimbabwean guerrillas fighting against the racist regime are just terrorists which is also the term accorded to them by both London and Salisbury. He is, in short, Fanon's quintessential colonised bourgeois, wasting precious time in 'sterile litanies and nauseating mimicry.'[21] He is a colonial ideal combining in himself a kind of Victorian morality mixed with the remnants of a decaying patriarchy, decaying because its real roots and base have already been undermined by colonialism, and a smugness that makes him insensitive to what is happening around him. He would turn everybody into a replica of himself just as the mission has turned him into a replica of itself. His

[20] Ibid., p. 54/54.
[21] Frantz Fanon, op. cit., p. 311

ideal for Tambudzai is when she is at the stage of seemingly accepting every colonial idiocy and irrelevant traditionalism he articulates. He had been moulded by the whites into their image of the good African – he had let himself be so moulded through never questioning anything – and in turn he would like to mould his family and those round him into colonial zombies after his likeness. They would become imitations of an imitation. The bourgeois whites who have moulded him into their image of the submissive African full of gratitude at white colonial charity appear to him as divinity. In the same way he reproduces himself as a divinity vis-à-vis those Africans under his care. This divinity, like its colonial father, is actually an embodiment of a self-serving piety, greed, and spiritual emptiness.

The greed is very well captured in one of the most terrifying scenes in the narrative: this is the scene earlier on in the story in which the women feed him.[22] He literally swallows dish after dish while the entire family watches him gorge himself to near sickness. He eats almost ten times more than he needs which of course means that he is eating food that could have fed more people. His food is snatched from the mouths of the hungry, his water from the mouths of the thirsty, symbolised in this instance, by the women and children around him. This is a colonial phenomenon since in precolonial cultures, children come first in the sharing out of scarce resources particularly food. The scene has echoes that go well beyond the Zimbabwean petty bourgeoisie to the Western bourgeoisie who burn food to boost profit when all around them are starving millions. The Western bourgeoisie also swallows more than 80 per cent of world resources. Consumerism becomes the aesthetic and moral ideal. The petty bourgeoisie is to the African masses what the Western bourgeoisie is to the global community. In the eating scene, the victims are mostly the women and children as is the case

[22] Dangarembga, op.cit., pp. 80-3/81-4.

in the global community. The scene is a celebration of negative materialism and it is reminiscent of the Latin American novel, particularly in the hands of Gabriel García Márquez.[23] In the midst of this greed he has time to moralise about sexual restraint and puritanism. D.H. Lawrence, in the Rhodesia of the sixties, is as horrifying to him as he had been to the remnants of the Victorian morality in England earlier. The discussion that follows his ban on D.H. Lawrence in his house has all the echoes of the Trial of *Lady Chatterley's Lover* in a Britain during the promiscuous culture of the sixties.

The emptiness in the spiritual mimicry is captured in the wedding at the church which he imposes on Jeremiah and his wife. Jeremiah is already legally married within his culture. He and his wife have grown-up children. So the new wedding requirements to mark their progress in the bourgeoisification process is a mockery of tradition and a mimicry of Christianity. Why a white wedding at the church? The white missionaries used to insist on such marriages and naming ceremonies as a way of symbolising the converts' complete break with their culture and their acceptance of white bourgeois customs. Since the title of the narrative is taken from Fanon, we can reasonably assume that Dangarembga shares the view of Christianity as described by Fanon: that 'the church in the colonies is a white people's church, the foreigner's church. It does not call the native to God's ways but to the ways of the whiteman, of the master. Of the oppressor.'[24] The colonial spiritual wasteland of Babamukuru's world also brings to mind the warning by Fanon at the conclusion of *The Wretched of the Earth*. There he warns Africa not to pay tribute to Europe by creating states and institutions and societies that drew their inspiration from Europe. Describing those imitations as obscene caricatures, he states words that could very well have been at the

---

[23] See Márquez's short story 'Big Mama's Funeral'.
[24] Frantz Fanon, op. cit., p. 42.

back of Dangarembga's mind in her conception of the character of Babamukuru: 'If we want to turn Africa into a new Europe ... then let us leave the destiny of our countries to Europeans. They will know how to do it better than the most gifted among us.'[25]

The white wedding at the church is clearly seen and depicted as an example of sterile imitations of Europe, a caricature of both the West and Africa.[26]

The ability to see through the spiritual wasteland is the beginning of wisdom and consequently political revolt. In *Nervous Conditions*, it is the women characters who are able to see through and make some tentative stands that indicate possibilities of spiritual renewal through rebellion. Tambudzai is in fact a keen observer who is able to spot the contradictions in Babamukuru's position. She also observes herself and is able to detect the changes that come over her as a result of her contact with the mission. Her earlier struggles for school against both her father and her brother had prepared her for this. She is also able to learn from her mother, from Nyasha, and from books. But the real turning point in distancing herself from Babamukuru's world comes about through her firm stand against attending her parents re-wedding at the church.

Nyasha is the most consistent critic of her father and of assimilation in general. Her breakdown is a recognition of the warring, irreconcilable forces within her, and also a revolt against both patriarchy and colonial culture. It is when she breaks down that she is best able to articulate what it is she is revolting against: the entire imitative culture of the African petty bourgeoisie. In their books, in their schools, in their colleges, in their churches,

---

[25] Ibid., p. 315.
[26] Some of these church practices that are clearly an imitation of the bourgeois aspects of white Christians are satirised in much African literature. But this particular practice of renewal of weddings is also treated in Ngũgĩ's story 'Wedding at the Cross' (1969) in *Secret Lives* and in Ngũgĩ's and Ngũgĩ's wa Mĩriĩ's *I Will Marry When I Want* (1976).

she sees only lies, what Sartre describes as these walking lies who no longer had anything to say to their brothers and sisters except echo London, Paris and Amsterdam. But her revolt exemplifies one of the forms that anti-colonial violence can take: internalised violence within the community and within self. For Fanon this internalised violence is just one of the stages in the long journey towards organised revolutionary violence against the colonial state. But it is one of the forms that revolt can take. Bulimia is an act of rebellion but it takes the destructive form of auto-violence or violation. The rebellion results in Nyasha being at her most articulate about colonial culture and its impact on the psyche of the colonised but the auto-violence results in the emaciation of her body. Not wanting to become one of the walking lies, she turns against herself. But the body and the mind succumb to the blow after blow of the self-violation and hence the *Anorexia Nervosa.*

It is interesting that it is the spiritually uncorrupted Tambu's mother who best articulates the destructive impact of the process of assimilation: she coins the term 'Englishness' and to her it is a disease. Thus when Nyasha and Chido come from England, she is able to see that they are suffering from Englishness. She detects the same disease in her son, Nhamo, and that's why she is able to foresee his death. The death of the spirit is clearly a precursor of the death of the flesh. When Nyasha breaks down Tambudzai's mother can see the effects of the same disease. To her the source of this disease is the mission place and abroad, and in this her outlook is at one with that of Frantz Fanon who sees institutional Christianity as waging war on embryonic heresies and even on evil as yet unborn, seeing the customs and myths and traditions of the colonised as the embodiment of evil. In fact we are given the impression that Tambudzai is finally saved because she heeds her mother's advice about Englishness. Reflecting on her mother's constant warnings, she asks herself:

Was I being careful enough? I wondered. For I was beginning to have a suspicion, no more than the seed of a suspicion, that I was too eager to leave the homestead and embrace the 'Englishness' of the mission; and after that the more concentrated 'Englishness' of the Sacred Heart. The suspicion remained for a few days, during which time it transformed itself into guilt, and then I had nightmares about Nhamo and Chido and Nyasha two nights in a row. That should tell you how much my mother's words disturbed me...[27]

In the system of colonial patriarchy, the system that produces males who are agents of the disease of Englishness, the women of all classes are collectively seen as the main victims. They suffer from what Tambudzai's mother calls their Femaleness. Maiguru, Babamukuru's wife is a case in point. She has the same level of formal education as her husband. She has in fact a Master's degree in philosophy. Yet her role in the world as described in *Nervous Conditions* is literally to reproduce, and to serve her husband. Nyasha whose social life is overregulated as compared to the freedom of social self-expression accorded to her brother is also seen as a victim of the same femaleness. So is Tambudzai who gets her chance of a place at the mission only after the death of her brother. But the suffering and sufferance are best symbolised by the position of Tambudzai's mother. She is a peasant, eking out a living from the soil. She is the one least spiritually corrupted, yet she is described as suffering from being 'female and poor and uneducated and black'.[28] She emerges as much more of a thinker than her husband, Jeremiah, but she always plays second fiddle to him. For most of her life, the narrator comments, 'my mother's mind, belonging first to her father and then to her husband, had not been hers to make up'.[29] She may be physically drained, resigned to her fate, but she is

---

[27] Dangarembga, op. cit., pp. 203/207.
[28] Ibid., pp. 89/91.
[29] Ibid., pp. 153/155.

very clear about colonial patriarchy and in her own way she is the one who best articulates the position of woman in that society. She does this when she is explaining to her sister, Lucia, why she has to fall in line with the Jeremiah's and Babamukuru's schemes of involving her in a second marriage ceremony where she has to pretend, at her age, that she is still a girl, a virgin, probably. She also explains the same things to Tambudzai in terms of the weight of womanhood on top of the poverty of her blackness. What she is describing are the three burdens which she as a peasant woman in a colonial society has to carry. As a peasant she is of course one with the rural poor and the urban poor. This class carries the burden of producing for the entire society and yet it gets very little in return. Middle-class women, like Maiguru, do not necessarily carry this burden. But she is also black and all black people are collectively victims of racism: hence the burden of her blackness which she shares with all black people, male or female, of whatever class. But she talks about the special burden of womanhood, and this is shared by all women irrespective of class and race and religion. In fact in the only active appearance of white characters, the white woman, Doris, is depicted as instinctively able to appreciate young Tambduzai's desires; and she is the one who comes up with the money that Tambudzai needs for school.

Given an oppressive system, what is to be done? The narrative seems to endorse the rightness of revolt. The most alive of the women are those who question and ultimately rebel. The impulses towards rebellion are exhibited by virtually every woman in the narrative. Tambudzai's mother, although the most physically impoverished, is also the most spiritually and even intellectually alive. Nyasha rebels against Babamukuru, at one time, going totally against tradition and hitting him. But she also uses the refusal to eat as a weapon of rebellion which is seen as counter-productive because she, unable to reconcile fully the forces warring inside her, suffers a mental breakdown, thereby eliminating herself from the struggle. The one moment when Maiguru becomes alive is when she gathers enough energy and leaves Babamukuru. And Tambudzai herself really comes of age after her rebellion; her refusal to attend her parents' second marriage ceremony. And finally Lucia: she is the embodiment of a free spirit, one that will not be tamed by any male authority. No marriage bonds except on her own terms. And when she decides to go back to school, to adult literacy classes, it is because she wants to improve her mental and spiritual well-being.

In her book, *Re-creating Ourselves*, Molara Ogundipe, talking about the many burdens that the African woman bears in a colonial and postcolonial society, argues that the most important is the woman herself:

> Women are shackled by their own negative self esteem, by centuries of interiorization of the ideologies of patriarchy and gender hierarchy. Their own reactions to objective conditions are therefore are often self defeating and self crippling. Woman reacts with fear, dependency complexes and attitudes to please and cajole where more self-assertive actions are needed.[30]

The women in *Nervous Conditions* exemplify, in their lives, the variants of the six mountains that Professor Molara Ogundipe talks about. But they are all shown as possessing the will and the capacity to assert themselves. It is also interesting that it is the women, and not the men, who are seen as rebelling. The rebellion of women against patriarchy is paralleled with and seen as an essential part of the entire colonial revolt. But this is implied rather than explored.

Thus, although the three burdens of race, class and gender that a woman has to bear are intertwined, the class and the race aspect are not as fully developed as the gender factor. The male characters

---

[30] Molara Ogundipe *Re-creating Ourselves* (Trenton: Africa World Press, 1994), p. 36.

are essentially variations of the same unchanging maleness. It is also the men who are on the whole carrier-agents of Westernism. All males of whatever class and age seem to behave in the same way. At least so in the drama of the domestic sphere. But part of the tensions in the narrative obviously emanate from the fact that a war is going on outside the domestic hearth, a war between the armed guerrillas of the liberation movements and the armed forces of the Rhodesian colonial regime. Except for one or two references to disagreements between Babamukuru and Nyasha about calling freedom fighters terrorists, it does not intrude into the action of the narrative. The actions, conflicts, clashes of outlook move on the domestic plane only, and this is both the strength and the weakness of the novel. On the strong side, the domestic sphere, the action literally oscillates between Babamukuru's home at the mission and Jeremiah's home in the village with much of the action taking place within the two centres – which gives a structural unity. It enables the ease of the narrative flow. The story unfolds through the eyes of a girl in her teens. Events domestic and public are seen through her eyes. The awareness of the public sphere, history and politics, remains at the level of the narrating consciousness. Again this consistent centre of awareness adds to the unity of theme, plot and atmosphere.

Limiting the point of view to that of the girl is also its weakness. Given the narrator's consciousness, it is obvious that what is happening in the domestic sphere will loom larger in her mind than even the greatest of earthquakes in the public sphere of politics and history. Hence too many questions are left unanswered. The period of the narrator's birth, childhood and teenhood are momentous for Zimbabwe. Between 1955 and 1965, the year of UDI, too many things have happened. The whites have formed a Federation with Northern Rhodesia which later breaks up. African political parties have been formed and as quickly banned by the colonial regime. Bus boycotts have taken place. African leaders are arrested, killed, imprisoned or forced into exile. Between 1961 and 1963, the three major parties that are to play the main roles in the unfolding historical drama had been formed: the Zimbabwe African People's Union in 1961, the Rhodesian Front, a right-wing white settler party, in 1962, and the Zimbabwe African National Union in 1963. Thus between UDI in 1965 and the Independence of Zimbabwe in 1980, it is war all the way. And with the UN imposing sanctions against the country, Rhodesia becomes an object of debate at the international level. Do none of these historical events intrude into the life of the narrator? What images of these forces form in the young people's minds? By pinpointing the years of certain fictional events, and by oblique references to UDI and to terrorists, the narrative invites these legitimate questions: what's happening out there? Surely people are dying and disappearing, there are soldiers in the streets: don't these events ever intrude into their lives? Has there never been a police raid, a white man stopping the character to demand to see their passes or anything?

Despite this, it is clear that *Nervous Conditions* is a political novel; and Tambudzai, the narrator, really comes of age when she begins to see the connections between patriarchy and colonialism and hence its dangers. In revolting against Babamukuru and what he stands for, the women are actually revolting against what is, in essence, a colonial creation. And really it is the Babamukurus of the colonial creation who, on assuming positions of power and authority in the postcolonial era, have wrought so much havoc on African societies. The novel provides the reasons why. They, the Babamukurus, think they owe whatever they have to the colonial system despite any amount of lip service they can give to Independence and African cultures. Most of them act as if it was really their co-operation with the colonial system – and not the actions of those terrorists – that really made the colonial master relinquish power. Thus the colonial master has left behind him a class made in his image, Fanon's 'black skins in white masks'. *Nervous Conditions* gives us a very insightful portrait of the mindset of this class: its genesis, formation and development in the test-tubes and greenhouses of colonial culture symbolised by the mission. Unfortunately it is the biological maleness of this class that is stressed and hence the determinism in the novel. The men are trapped in their biological maleness and hence what they do is rooted in biology rather than history. The problem with any deterministic philosophy is that in the end it exonerates the victimisers: if human beings act the way they do because of their biological make up, or because they are fated to do what they do, then they cannot be held morally accountable for their actions. It is in their nature to do what they do. But patriarchy is not a biological phenomenon rather a historical phenomenon and so it can also be altered by human actions of both men and women. This is also true of racism and all racist ideologies which can be altered through human struggles. The real challenge of the African narrative is whether or not it is able to treat meaningfully the interplay of class, gender, race and religion in the quest for a new human sensibility.

However in many anti-colonial texts, including Fanon's, there is too much silence over gender politics. It is an aspect of colonialism and anti-colonial revolt which is not often consistently examined in the African narratives of the colonial or post-colonial era. Hence the importance of *Nervous Conditions* and the body of literature that is increasingly being produced by women of Africa and the world.

Index

Printed and bound by CPI Group (UK) Ltd, Croydon, CR0 4YY

13/04/2025

14656523-0002